> Emma,
> All at
> Universe ......
> to you, my darling,
> and to your family.
> The Author
> Dora Klimove
> Nov. 2016

Did You Ever Have the Chance to Marry an American Multimillionaire?

Did You Ever Have the Chance to Marry an American Multimillionaire?

Dora Klinova

Copyright © 2016 Dora Klinova
All rights reserved. No part of this book maybe reproduced or transmitted in any form or by any means whatsoever without written permission from the author.

ISBN: 1533137854
ISBN 13: 9781533137852

Edited by Barbara Villaseñor

Dora Klinova

www.doraklinova.com

dorishka2000@yahoo.com

Please, direct your opinion, comments and inquiries to:

DK Corporation
5712 Baltimore Drive, Unit 461
La Mesa, CA 91942
Tel. (619) 667-0925

Is This Your Story?

THREE MONTHS AFTER arriving in America from the Soviet Union, which was falling apart at the time, in her mid-fifties and lacking English, Della finds herself in a serious romantic relationship with a handsome American who appears to be a multimillionaire. How does she handle this opportunity? Can Della pull it off? Does she really want to?

This real life adventure is filled with many surprising, joyous, funny and, alas, tragic twists and turns. It is told in a very spicy, direct and intimate way, focusing sometimes on racy developments.

The story is told not only as a universal drama for all aspiring ladies looking for their Mr. Wonderful, but is sprinkled with philosophical diamonds about what life is really all about.

How does it all work out? Can her man perform to his and her satisfaction? We can't tell it here, you've got to read this high level romance novel yourself. And along the way, keep your eyes gazing upward, since The Master, God, guides the plot, Della and her Herbert, Mr. Wonderful, the drama's main protagonists.

This could become the model for Everyone hoping to find meaning in their own life's pot-boiler of an adventure story.

Cyril Roseman, Ph.D.

In the memory of

Harold Steckel

Nothing is truly learned until it is lived"

-THE WAY OF THE WIZARD-

The problem with life is that the test comes first and the lesson after.

Introduction

EXTREMELY UNBELIEVABLE AND extremely true story! This unique incredible experience is not a fairytale.

We all know how unpredictable life can be in reality. Life is an exciting adventure, a great performance and we play our roles in it without any idea what we are supposed to do in the following act. We don't know what the next moment will bring.

Everything you will read here is based on real facts and woven out of the threads of personal experience. All participants in this story are real people.

To start the story let us imagine that it happened to you. You are my best friend, your name is Della Gordon, you told me your story in detail, and I produced an exciting bestseller from your life.

I would like to introduce Della Gordon. She came to the United States in her late fifties as a Jewish refugee from the falling apart USSR. Before departure, she divorced her husband, survived numerous serious surgeries, was nearly on her deathbed, endured a lot of pain, and arrived in the United States with a disability certificate.

Della went through an unusual exciting experience that turned into a huge leap to the highest strata of American society. Her great sense of humor helped her tremendously. Della is a very bright, full of light and love person. She doesn't hide her fear and shows no bitterness or anger, only courage and hope.

All of Della's tender, touching story—her struggles in the Soviet Union, her challenges as an immigrant here, and her Cinderella romance—intrigued me. Her passion for life, to learn life's lessons, especially caught my attention. I see her story as a statement of a generous, forgiving and loving woman.

She asked me to make her experiences come alive, but to change the names, the more so the main participants in this story have already left this world. Hopefully, they are in heaven now and their spirits are helping Della to fully express herself on these pages.

Her story is a wonderful, romantic love song between two people who met each other in their mature age. They both were amazed how these deep, incredible feelings could arise in their souls. There was so much kindness in Della's experience and so many temptations. There was a mixture of love and envy, understanding and harm, as well as so much spite and evil directed toward her that she asked me to begin this novel with a prayer from the Bible.

"Our Father in heaven,
Hallowed be Your name,
Your Kingdom come,
Your Will be done,
On earth as it is in heaven.
Give us this day our daily bread.
And forgive us our debts,
As we forgive our debtors.
And do not lead us into temptation,
But deliver us from the evil one.
For Yours is the Kingdom and the
Power and the Glory forever."
The New Testament. Matthew 6:9

You, my dear reader, are welcome to enjoy Della's story and to derive much wisdom for yourself here.

Dora Klinova, the writer

CHAPTER 1

Did you ever have the chance to marry an American multimillionaire? Della Gordon would like to ask you this question. You did not? She did. And no one was more astonished than Della. Really, not every day an American multimillionaire appears in your life, especially if you are already 56 and have just come as a poor Jewish refugee from the alien world of the Soviet Union.

Exactly three months after arriving in the United States the miracle happened: a real American multimillionaire came into Della's life. She became his Princess. Moreover, she became his Queen.

Della was sure it was God's will to send him to her and it also was God's will to send Della to him. At that period of his life, he was exhausted and down, and, like a blessing and full of joy, he met Della. Many thanks to You, dear God!

This is not a Cinderella fairytale. This is real life, more remarkable than any fantasy. Life has its own twists. Extraordinary things can happen to us when an Omnipotent Magician turns our wheel of fortune in an unpredictable direction.

On July 20, 1992 Della came to the United States from the Soviet Union, which had just collapsed. She brought with her advanced age, a recently broken right arm and shoulder, her body and mind falling apart from all the tension of immigration, and fear of a new life in a foreign country.

Instead of a husband, she came with a terrific substitute: her barely alive, half blind, half deaf, 83-year-old Aunt Rachel, wheelchair bound. An invalid with a broken, unhealed hip since 1982, Rachel sat regally in her wheelchair as if seated on a throne, holding her two crutches in her arms like two grand czar's scepters.

This was Della's glorious, victorious arrival to the United States of America!

They were allowed to bring only two pieces of luggage and two hundred dollars per person. A full year before departure Della thought, "How can I squeeze my whole life in the USSR into two suitcases?" She made it. She thrust her and her aunt's lifetime into four suitcases. It was all their property. The essential ingredients were two big pillows, two blankets, six thick cotton sheets and enamelware pots. Somebody had assured her that America had a huge shortage of bedding and pots.

Della was smart. Instead of four hundred dollars for both of them, she brought six hundred. Two hundred dollars she concealed in a coffee can under the coffee. Because of this illegal action, the customs examination made her extremely nervous. She was afraid that the customs official, right in the middle of her exam, would have the urgent desire to taste Soviet coffee from this particular can. He skipped this desire. Therefore Della felt saved, plus the secret additional $200 gave her a feeling of great security in America.

Della and Rachel arrived in San Diego. Jewish Family Services greeted them. Their workers were very supportive and tried to help as much as possible. A one-bedroom apartment, furnished pretty well, was prepared for them. They told Della that all the furniture was donated to Jewish Family Services by other people. So Della's first impression was that Americans were very generous people for donating such good quality furniture and other things needed in daily life.

Their apartment was big, located in a secured complex with a swimming pool. In Odessa, a few years before departure to America, Della moved to a new area, but there were no pools near apartment buildings. They did not build swimming pools in Odessa.

Very early in the morning Della rushed to the pool. She jumped and sang, looking with joy into California's blue sky.

"God, dear God, am I in America? Can I swim here in this blue pool under blue sky whenever I want? Am I really in America?"

She asked this aloud, raising her arms to the heavens. Then she dove into the pool and swam, trying to wash out her tiredness and her overwhelming emotional strain.

Did You Ever Have the Chance to Marry an American Multimillionaire?

"I made it! I made it! I broke through an enormous barrier of huge obstacles, struggles and fights, not only for myself, but for old Rachel! Amazing! I did it! My God, I did it!"

She touched the walls of the pool, splashed the water, swam back and forth, whispering and singing again and again:

"I made it! I made it! I did the impossible! No, it was not me. Dear God, You made it! Thank you, God!"

She did not have all the words to fully express her incredible gratitude. She had not yet heard the expression "God bless America!" But when she did, she repeated these three words thousands of times for everything that was given to her in this new country.

During the first few weeks, they were sent tons of letters and applications and had to appear at hundreds of appointments, especially Aunt Rachel. It seemed that America was solely and persistently focused only on the needs of her handicapped aunt.

Day and night Della sat at the table covered with letters and English-Russian dictionaries, trying hard to understand with her poor English what America wanted of them.

She could spend sleepless nights filling out all the applications, but it was impossible for her to take the handicapped aunt to appointments because she didn't drive and, of course, didn't have a car.

Jewish Family Services kindly sent volunteers to help them. One of them, Jacob, telephoned Della and said that he was ready to take Rachel to a doctor for her hearing aid. Della made arrangements with him and when the time came, she brought Rachel in the wheelchair downstairs to the gate of their apartment building. They waited for Jacob in the hot sun for a long time.

Rachel started to yell at Della:

"I demand to be taken back upstairs! Now!"

Ever since arriving in America, her aunt's demeanor had changed. She had become a shrew. In Rachel's eyes Della was a servant she could boss around.

Jacob finally showed up. He was so handsome that Rachel immediately stopped yelling. He introduced himself in Russian manner: Yasha. He told

Della that he was studying the Russian language as well as the Torah. Della laughed.

"Why are you laughing?" Yasha asked.

"Please, forgive me, Yasha. Russian and Torah are so 'related' subjects. It is funny you study them together."

So excited was Jacob to be able to practice speaking Russian, that he talked on and on, forgetting about the purpose of his visit. After listening to Jacob speak "Russian" demonstrating his "knowledge" for what seemed like a long time, Della couldn't contain herself any more. Besides, she couldn't understand a word he was saying in his "Russian". "Yasha, please," Della interrupted, "let's go to the appointment. We are late, and we can speak as we drive."

After the doctor's visit Della invited him to her apartment for dinner. She prepared Russian borsch, which is soup with vegetables and red beets. He said that he was an Orthodox Jew and ate only kosher food. It surprised her because he looked so modern, with a short haircut and with a good-looking, clean-shaven face.

Jacob asked Della, "Are the ingredients of your dinner kosher?"

Della had only a vague notion what kosher food was. "I don't know," she shrugged. "I bought the biggest, cheapest chicken I could find at the market, and the vegetables are very nice, too."

Jacob was probably so hungry and so interested in talking with an intelligent woman who had just recently arrived from Russia, that he decided to forget all kosher restrictions and agreed to have dinner with them. He reminded her of herself in Odessa, desperate to speak 'real American' English with anyone she could find.

He liked her borsch with supermarket chicken. Della felt that he probably hadn't eaten good home-cooked food for ages and gave him a second serving. He ate it with gusto. Perhaps later he prayed to God to forgive him the sin of enjoying non-kosher food.

Jacob started to discuss very specific points about the Torah in detail, mixing Russian and English words. He didn't want to waste his time; he wanted to improve his knowledge of the Russian language on the spot. To

Did You Ever Have the Chance to Marry an American Multimillionaire?

be honest, Della had never even seen a Torah in her life. The practice of Judaism was forbidden in the Soviet Union, so she knew very little about her religion. Nevertheless, she made what she thought were very intelligent and significant comments in their conversation.

She didn't know how they talked because her English was awful and his Russian was so 'advanced' that she preferred his English. Anyway, their conversation was so long that he stayed on that first visit until 12 midnight, leaving her deadly exhausted.

He called every day, talking for hours on the telephone in his 'Russian'. She didn't understand a word and asked him to translate it into English, which she also didn't understand. She tried her best to help him with his Russian, even though she had a headache after their conversations and felt a great relief when he hung up.

Jacob was delighted with Della's company. He liked her very much and was no longer interested in taking old Aunt Rachel to see doctors as an excuse to be with Della. So, he quit being a volunteer at Jewish Family Services when he became Della's admirer. They were very connected. He was the first American person with whom she could speak openly about everything, asking him thousands of questions about American culture, customs, people, etc.

One day, during one of their chats, Della surprised herself and asked him:

"Is it true there are stores in America where they sell special devices for sex?"

"Yes! Actually one of them is not too far from your home. Would you like to see it?"

"No. What are you talking about? I was just curious. Of course not. No, no! It is a shame that you ask me to go there! No! Y-e-e-s! I want to see it. Why not?" she murmured.

"Let's go!"

"Right now?"

"Yes, of course!"

Her mind became confused. *What did I do? I have such a big mouth!*

She went with him to his car and felt like a teenager about to do something improper. Her curiosity overpowered her sense of decency.

He brought her into an X-rated sex store—'F-Street'—with all its exciting 'do-dads'. She really hadn't seen anything like this in her whole life and wanted to escape from the shop as soon as possible, if not sooner. To tell the truth, she was very interested to see all the 'equipment' and 'appliances' for sex, but the store was full of people. Della was surprised how popular this place was, plus, her modest Russian upbringing didn't permit her to look at these things and investigate them in detail, especially in the presence of a young, handsome American man. She was ashamed even to look at the shelves.

"Let us watch a movie in a private room!" he said to Della.

"Right now?" she asked for the second time that day.

"Yes, right now. Choose, please, the most exiting sexual movie that you would like to see."

Can you imagine? An Orthodox Jew suggesting Della and he watch a porno movie together in the private room of a sex shop? She looked at the shelf with a pile of porno DVDs. Did Jacob ask her to choose the best? She never watched any in her life; what did she know?

She refused his offer. Why did Della behave so cowardly? In her mature age, what difference did it make? She didn't know, but she was ashamed like a little girl. She was sure that more Torah study would help Jacob behave in this delicate situation.

"Come on, Della, what are you afraid of?" he insisted.

"I am not afraid." Della played herself a brave girl. "I am just not accustomed to do this."

"Della, please, relax, you are in America, let us have some fun." the Orthodox Jew said.

"You are in America, not me."

"Wait a minute," he looked at Della with big eyes. "Where are you now?"

"I am here, but my mind didn't arrive to America yet, it is still attached to the Soviet customs."

Did You Ever Have the Chance to Marry an American Multimillionaire?

Della's smart theoretical answer sounded so boring and not appropriate in this situation. But she said firmly:

"NO! Not now. Next time."

She was smart enough to understand that the next time will never come, but stupidly repeated: "NO!"

Later on she wanted to see this store on her own just for fun, but she couldn't find it. However, by the time she became more familiar with San Diego and she knew where the store was, she had lost the curiosity to pursue this matter further. *We must act on the moment and do everything at the correct time,* she mused. *If we delay something, we lose the sense and the excitement of that particular adventure which life offers us spontaneously. We should never postpone the moment. Grab the opportunity and enjoy it. Right now!*

Della couldn't forgive herself that she lost what she thought was such an exciting opportunity. It was her terrible mistake, one she hoped she wouldn't make again.

Maybe, some of you, dear readers, are surprised:

"Why is she revealing such private things? It is a shame!"

Oh, yes! You are right. Is it not good to open up our true feelings; is it better to hide them? If you read anything in these pages that disturbs you, something too private, please, simply modestly close your eyes.

By the way, have you had any experiences in your life that you would prefer not to talk about? You have, haven't you?

Please, whisper it in my ear, I adore hearing it. And do you know why? Because there is no doubt that these moments have been precisely your real life.

After this adventure, Jacob offered to show Della the office where he worked. He rented a room there for his business. The room was small, but the office was very large. Jacob showed Della a conference room with a large table, chairs, and a big comfortable sofa.

The office was empty; everyone had gone home for the day. And the sofa was really spacious and cozy. And it happened. Yes, they both were too excited after visiting the porno store and it did happen. Jacob became Della's lover. Honestly, she did not resist. She was too curious to taste the American aroma of making love. So, she tried it. Jacob expanded Della's American experience, but she was not infatuated too much. Nothing special. In this delicate situation men and women do not show their citizenship certificates; they are just human beings, males and females, with their natural desire of lovingly comforting each other and being together. Yes, Della felt comfortable with Jacob, with his young robust body, but she knew that this relationship would not last long.

CHAPTER 2

Jacob worked in the insurance business. He mentioned that his landlord, a nice Jewish man, had just recently lost his wife. He was in grief and perhaps, Jacob suggested, it would be a good idea for Della to talk to him and to bring some fresh air into his life. Next, Jacob told his landlord that he had met an attractive, intelligent lady from Russia. The landlord became interested in meeting this intelligent lady.

"I am new here," Della told Jacob. "You will do a kind thing if you bring nice people into my life."

"Well, we can do it, but he is not for you, he is much older," Jacob said.

"It doesn't mean that it will become a relationship, but if he is an interesting person, why not meet him?"

"How about us and our relationship?" Jacob asked.

"Jacob, dear, you are wonderful. But I am much older. You are a young man. Your age is perfectly okay with me, but my age is not for you. You need to find a younger woman. Our relationship wouldn't work. We are good friends, aren't we? What can be wrong if we go together with your landlord to a lunch?" Della said.

The landlord pushed Jacob to introduce Della to him, probably because Jacob looked so excited while talking with him about her.

Even though it had been his idea to make the introductions, Jacob wasn't in a hurry. He was a divorcee; he felt comfortable with Della, and he didn't want to lose her. A month went by. She teased him that he was such an 'outstanding' matchmaker. Eventually, he told Della that his landlord would like to invite her for lunch at noon the next day.

She had an English class at that time. She promised herself she would never miss any English classes, but what class could compare with the opportunity to be introduced to a nice man, especially an American Jew and a landlord? She debated with herself about breaking her promise. Then, she reasoned: *Go, forget about your college class, you will have live English conversation. This will be your lesson. You will have real American English talk.*

Della felt good about her decision and thanked Jacob for moving the matchmaking along. She acted cheerful, but inside she felt confused. She had only been in America three months and her English was very poor. She was also a little bit shy. How to behave with these Americans? How to talk with them?

Della asked Jacob for help. She joked: "If you became a matchmaker, please, do it completely. Join us for lunch. You should promise me your emotional support in our conversation and I will help you so much with your Russian lessons that you will speak like President Gorbachev." They made a deal, laughing at this situation; he guaranteed his help.

He brought Della to the same office where she had already been. The landlord waited for them. Standing in the office was a tall, handsome man in a white hat. "Herbert Samson. Pleased to meet you," he presented himself, looking directly into Della's eyes. Then he took her hand, gave a nod to Jacob that meant "I don't need you anymore", and led her out the building. She didn't even have enough time to look attentively at him.

Mr. Samson put Della in his fine, red Cadillac. Then, assuming Della would understand him better, he spoke to her in Yiddish. The first thing he told her was that he had money and that she would not need to work.

Mr. Samson acted so quickly that it caught Della off balance. She finally came to herself, noticing that it was much nicer to sit in this Cadillac than in Jacob's half broken, rusty van.

It is a good change, she joked to herself, *but Jacob is much younger than the landlord. This is not a good change for me.*

Della smiled inside: *Did Mr. Samson mention something about his money? Why? He wants me to like him more, to be more interested in him? Who knows? Was it a promise to feed me if I would faint from hunger in America? It seems to me that I heard this hint in his voice. Okay, we will see.*

CHAPTER 3

They ate lunch at Marie Callender's on Alvarado Road sitting in a booth in a quiet place. Della looked at the menu. Herbert could see that she was having trouble making up her mind what to order. Della didn't understand anything on the menu. He ordered chicken pies for both of them, the specialty of the house.

They looked at each other and talked. Della was curious about his age. He intuitively felt it and showed his driver's license. This detail was important for her. He was open and wasn't trying to hide anything.

Della looked at his date of birth. May 3, 1922. He was a Taurus, she was a Capricorn. A perfect astrological match. He was 70, fourteen years older than she was. The difference in age was not so terrible. It made her feel better and also more relaxed; they started to talk with confidence to each other. They both felt an immediate connection.

Even though they had been born and had lived their lives in different countries and cultures, they felt like they had known each other for centuries. He told her about his life; she spoke about hers. Probably this confidence and connection helped Della calm down, because English words flew from her mouth. She forgot that she was speaking in a foreign language; she thought only about him and her.

They talked about everything and understood each other very well. When people feel connected, the language doesn't matter.

Something occurs between them that is much more valuable than words.

Herbert told her that he had lost his wife five months ago. She was 15 years older than he was. When he married her, he was 25 and she was 40. Della was good in math and quickly made the calculation in her head: they married in 1947. Della was just twelve.

Herbert was a poor young man before marriage. She owned a jewelry store. In the late forties, a jewelry store was great wealth. She had three children: a seventeen-year-old boy Al, a six-year-old daughter Donna, and a baby son, two-year-old Clint. Herbert adopted Donna and Clint; Al was already big enough and didn't want to be adopted. Herbert lived with his wife 43 years and raised her children.

What forced Herbert, a young, handsome fellow, to marry a woman fifteen years older with three children? He said he loved her. Who knows? Life is strange; we never know what is really going on in anyone's soul. For sure, he really loved her and was happy, or, maybe, her jewelry store played an important role in that love and marriage. It was none of Della's business.

She told him that in the Soviet Union she worked for many years as an engineer-designer in the movie industry. He looked at her with admiration.

"An engineer? In the movie industry? How did you make it in the Soviet Union, being a Jew?"

"It is a long story to tell, but, yes, I made it. It was an interesting job; I enjoyed it. In order to continue the engineering career here, in America, I must know English, computers, and be able to drive. I have none of these skills. At that time the engineers in the Soviet Union didn't use computers. We designed with a pencil! It was our main tool.

Being an engineer in the USSR, I couldn't afford to buy a car. I am not able to drive. Now I am in America. At my age it is too late to start an engineering career here. I must forget about that and concentrate on studying English. Then I will see how life unfolds."

Then it occurred to Della. "Today is October 20th, exactly three months since I arrived in this country," Della exclaimed. "A special day for me."

"A special day for me, too," said Herbert. "It is the day I met you."

Herbert again mentioned that Della didn't need to worry about anything because he had money. He affirmed that he liked her very much and would support her all her life. The second time she was surprised by his words. She liked what she heard, but deep inside, she didn't trust him. She knew that promises made so easily could be quickly forgotten.

Did You Ever Have the Chance to Marry an American Multimillionaire?

After lunch Herbert brought Della back to her apartment building. She felt that if she invited him in now, he would be very glad to come. But she didn't want to do it for fear that Herbert would run away immediately upon seeing her handicapped aunt. Della didn't know how they would find her at that moment. So she thanked him for lunch. He repeated that he liked her very much, promised to call soon, and left.

At home Della digested the meeting, Herbert, their conversation, and the chicken pie.

So, she thought, *he looked smart, intelligent, and polite. Plus, he is very handsome, tall, and shapely. Being a recent widower, he wasn't spoiled by women. He looked depressed, which was normal for having lost his wife only five months ago. I am 56; he is 70. Yes, 14 years was not a big difference in age.*

In her opinion, physical age was not so important. What's more important was how the person feels inside. He looked energetic and open to any changes in his life.

Della felt his deep tiredness. He had been near his sick, old, cancer-ridden wife for too long a time. She knew that period in his life was very hard for him. Della lived with her old, sick aunt and also felt exhausted. Again and again a question appeared in her mind: *Why did he immediately mention his money at the first moment of our meeting? Was it his main selling point?*

That Herbert had money was perfectly okay with Della. But why did he tell her about it so soon, repeating it several times? It was a little bit strange to her. Who understands these Americans? Is it very important for them to introduce their financial status along with their name?

He was 70 years old. Was he able to make love? She hoped, because he was an American. In her imagination, American men were supposed to be vigorous until 100. Time will tell. He will call.

CHAPTER 4

HE DIDN'T CALL. Several days passed, then a week, then 10 days. There were no calls. Jacob was surprised; he didn't know what happened because Herbert thanked him very sincerely for introducing him to Della.

She consoled herself: *He doesn't want to call, it is okay; the problem is his, not mine.*

She tried to forget him. She was too busy arranging everything for herself, for her old aunt, and their new life in America. She didn't want to think about him; she didn't have time.

Finally, two weeks later he called. He explained that he struggled with himself all that time. He had lived with his wife 43 years and forgot when he last dated a woman. It was difficult for him to overcome this barrier. Della understood his feelings.

He asked her, "Would you give me your kind permission to invite you to the Hotel Del Coronado for lunch with me?"

Della took a deep breath. Although she was only three months in America, she knew already that the Hotel Del Coronado was an expensive, prestigious, and special place in San Diego.

Hmm ...Herbert decided to show me America in all its beauty and chic. Wonderful! I will accept his invitation, Della thought.

Herbert's stock went up in Della's eyes. She kindly agreed to go with him to the Hotel Del Coronado.

The next day he arrived in a beautiful white new Lincoln. It was almost as big as a limousine. They drove across the Coronado Bridge. A kind, polite American Jewish man was with her, a splendid, white car, a calm ocean, clear blue sky, bright sun, seagulls, white yachts, a magic view from the bridge. She couldn't believe it was real. She talked with herself:

Life is so beautiful, you are in America. Breathe freely and enjoy this terrific moment. You are in paradise.

Did You Ever Have the Chance to Marry an American Multimillionaire?

As much as she tried to derive pleasure from every little thing that appeared before her eyes, she could not do it. Her mind compared "then and now." And although Della was deeply impressed by everything she saw in America, she was unable to forget the past. *We can take ourselves out of the country, but we cannot take the country out of ourselves,* she mused.

Three months—it was such a small amount of time to digest so many changes. Too much had happened in too little time to take this grandiosity in a normal way. Outwardly, she was calm and quiet, but inside she felt a storm of delight and a tempest of indignation that her life in the Soviet Union had been so terribly wasted.

People have limits, Della reflected. *It appears that we experience stress not only when our situation changes from good to bad. We also feel stressed when we find ourselves in an extremely good place after long suffering.*

As they drove up to the entrance of the Hotel Del Coronado, Della's eyes danced with excitement. To see this elegant, white graceful building with its distinctive red roof, the beautiful landscape and the white sand beaches beyond, delighted Della.

The valet opened the door to the white gorgeous Lincoln and took Della's hand to help her out. Herbert came around the car and hooked his arm into her elbow, leading her up the wide steps into the grand hotel and into the lobby.

Eating a delicious lunch in the Crown Room, Della looked at the beautiful decoration on its old walls and ceiling. She knew how many famous people had visited this place. Now she was here. God gave her this opportunity. God decided that she deserved it. Overwhelmed, Della gaily chatted with Herbert; inside she felt tense as a coiled spring. Oh, it was such a hard time. She felt like she was in two places at once. *We can physically put ourselves in a new country, in different unfamiliar situations, but emotionally we still continue to be in the old site. Our mentality is very conservative; it stubbornly resists. We need time to accept a new reality and feel comfortable in a new place.*

They walked on the beach arm-in-arm and continued talking. Then Herbert drove her back home, said many nice things, and left. Della knew that Herbert was waiting for her invitation.

She prepared a good Russian meal and called him:

"It is my turn now. Would you like to come for lunch?"

"Oh, sure, with great pleasure!"

His voice was happy. He appeared with a big bouquet of red roses. While she made something in the kitchen, Herbert entertained Aunt Rachel on the balcony, trying to make up a conversation with her. He behaved like a gentleman. Aunt Rachel, half deaf, didn't understand any English. He yelled, mixing Yiddish and English words, amusing her with political news. The weather was very hot; Rachel mentioned something about the absence of rain, which in Yiddish is 'regen'. Herbert didn't know Yiddish well and thought that she was talking about President Reagan. At that moment, Herbert's mind tuned to the White House in Washington. Now he explained to her in detail why Mr. Reagan was not in power anymore. Rachel didn't understand a word, but "took up his ideas," complaining with authority about 'regen-rain'. They both were sure they were discussing the same subject. Listening to them in the kitchen, Della was choking with laughter.

Della thought that in this way people can make a conversation in any language. Everybody discusses his own subject. Who cares? It is not necessary to understand one other. You can just have fun expressing your thoughts and enjoying this process.

They ate the lunch in leisure. Herbert liked her food, repeating "delicious, delicious." Della watched him; he became relaxed and looked satisfied. His face was not tense anymore; his wrinkles became softer, he looked content. She felt that he cherished his soul in her home. She was so glad to help her new friend to release his inner stress. She knew that it was the most important thing his heart needed and desired right now, at this moment. They talked a long time and had very warm feelings about each other.

CHAPTER 5

They started dating. Herbert was smart and polite and behaved like a real gentleman. It was a delight to talk with him. Even though he was born and lived in America, he also had hard times in his life. Della felt his good heart and loneliness. They liked each other and felt so comfortable together. He listened to her problems and became her first adviser and counselor. His life experience was so helpful; his emotional support grew important for Della. She was too tired to fight her way in this New World on her own.

Della was proud and grateful to have Herbert beside her. The previous part of her life in the USSR was over. Now it was time for her life to really begin.

On November 20th, when Herbert picked Della up, he presented her with a beautiful bouquet of roses. "Today marks the first month of our special relationship. We shall celebrate at Marie Callendar's."

Surprised that he remembered the exact date, Della could feel her heart open and was very touched by his sentimentality.

"Our day of appreciation," Della said, hugging the flowers to her chest.

"May we celebrate this day for a very long time," said Herbert, smiling affectionately at Della.

After they had dated for a while, Della became curious about one thing. Herbert didn't attempt even to kiss her. She wondered how he would do it. Who knows, maybe here in America it is a different approach. In the beginning Della was patient, then she started to tease him. She teased him so much that finally, after a dinner out, he parked the car in front of the gate of her apartment building and leaned across the seat, drew her near, and kissed her. It was still light outside; she didn't want to do this in front of her neighbors.

"Herbert, people will see us!" He was all flushed as he drove a little bit farther away, parked, and continued to kiss her.

She liked him very much and kissed him back with all her passion. He was shocked. When he got his breath back, he asked in amazement, "Wow! How do you know to kiss a man so good? I love it. Where did you learn?"

Della replied, laughing, "I would be ashamed of myself if I didn't know how to do it at my age." Then she added, "It is Russian style."

He wanted sex immediately, right there in the car.

"Forty-three years ago I *screwed* my wife for the first time in the car. It was delicious!"

He wanted to repeat that delightful experience from his youth and to feel himself young again. Why shouldn't he? Della was amazed how Herbert, an elderly man, turned into a young boy with excited eyes when he was with her. She looked at him with admiration.

"I did a good job with you, didn't I?" she asked him, laughing.

"Oh, yes! Certainly! You are a great woman! You are a terrific lady. First time in my life I met a woman like you!"

Feeling confused and ashamed, Della said, "Listen, it is still light outside, people are walking right near us. Can we have a little bit of privacy?" Della could not ignore her modest Soviet upbringing and knew she could not continue in the car.

This made their situation very complicated. Where could they go? She couldn't invite Herbert to her apartment because Rachel occupied the only bedroom; Della slept in the living room, and her aunt could destroy their privacy at any moment. Della couldn't send her anywhere from home, for example to the movie theater. Rachel's biggest journey was a trip from the bed to the toilet. Sometimes she "went out" from her bed and came to the living room to watch TV.

And Della couldn't ask Rachel to stay in her bedroom and keep the door closed, because immediately Rachel would ask, "Why?" If Della

Did You Ever Have the Chance to Marry an American Multimillionaire?

would explain "why", Rachel would be very disappointed in Herbert and her opinion of him would plummet. Rachel never was married and in her 83 years she was still a virgin. When sometimes she noticed that a man simply hugged Della, she felt compelled to teach Della how she should behave with men.

Even so, Della loved her aunt and didn't want to hurt her feelings or make her uncomfortable.

Herbert's situation was also intricate. He owned a condo not so far away, but he lived with a housekeeper.

He told Della, "I cannot do it at home, she is always there."

Della admonished him:

"What is the problem? Who is the boss? Tomorrow give her a day off."

"Impossible; she lives in Mexico, she doesn't have any place to go."

Della replied, "So, give her money to take a bus and let her see San Diego. She would be happy."

Della didn't know what agreement Herbert made with his housekeeper, but the next day he brought her to his condo. They both waited impatiently for this cherished moment of privacy. Herbert told Della that he hadn't slept the whole night worrying and thinking about their forthcoming intimate date. He was worn out with that sleepless night.

Della felt both shy and excited as he embraced her and led her into his bedroom. Finally they had their privacy. The room was heavily curtained and very dim, as they hurriedly undressed and then got into bed together. He wanted her so much and ... he couldn't do it. He was very disappointed; she was upset also. Even her passionate kisses did not do their magic this time.

Some women know this terrible feeling when they are in love, have a strong desire, and their man cannot do anything. Now Della was sorry that she didn't let him do it in the car the day before. Maybe his ability would have been stronger and she wouldn't be so frustrated. It was the second time in the past few months that she had the thought, *Why postpone any exciting event that life offers to us at this particular moment?*

CHAPTER 6

In Russia, Della had a vague idea about America. In her imagination American men were supposed to be muscular sportsmen with big arms and legs, and very good at making love. She was optimistic, she believed in America and in American men.

Della left, convincing herself not to worry. *Be patient with him. He will come to himself. You will awake him. Of course you will. And besides that, it is America, they do wonders here.*

Meeting people, we do not know what they look like in private. Mr. Samson, an owner of a big shopping center in San Diego, a respected businessman, appeared in front of Della in his underwear. His underpants were long, down to his knees, and showed his two thin, stick-like legs. Della saw men in similar underpants in American movies from the 1920s. Her sense of humor immediately created funny thoughts in her head: *My God, why did you send me a man from the last century? He is a relic, a representative from ancient times. If all American men are like him, I will run away back to Russia. Better I would live there as a refugee from America.* Herbert, a very handsome man, did not pay any attention to his underwear; he just did not care. His wife, being much older and sick, did not care also. Della felt with all her heart how Herbert was lonesome and how desperately he needed a woman's caress and attention. She understood she must shower him with love.

How could she ask Herbert to change underwear in a polite way without offending him?

"Herbertchik, can we please each other with good looking underwear? Do you know a store where they sell gorgeous underwear, for men and for women?"

"Sure, Dellishka, but to tell you the truth, I didn't buy underwear for centuries. I didn't buy clothes for myself, only for my wife."

"Why not for yourself also?"

Did You Ever Have the Chance to Marry an American Multimillionaire?

"I was not interested."

"And now?"

"Oh, yes, I am."

So he took Della to K-Mart.

"Choose whatever you want," he said generously. Della was happy; she came with an American man to an American store where everything was supposed to be perfect quality. But she did not see any gorgeous underwear there. At that time she didn't know the difference between K-Mart and Victoria's Secret. She chose some for herself, not many, but Herbert did not even look at man's stuff. She asked him:

"Would you like to buy new underpants for yourself?"

"No, I have plenty of them. I don't need any."

"You mean what you wear now?"

"Yes, they are comfortable."

"Would you like to try another one for a change?"

"What am I supposed to do with my own?"

"Do you have a garbage can in your house?"

He learned quickly. Della never saw him again in his old-fashioned underwear.

Herbert called every day inviting her somewhere. She accepted his invitations with big pleasure. Immigration problems exhausted her and she was glad to run away from the endless routine at home. The more so, he showed her the most exotic, fancy and expensive places in San Diego. This gave Della the belief that he really had money. He asked her to go out again and again. Often she was deadly tired, but somehow the energy came back to her.

Herbert was tremendously happy. He was so much in need of a fresh flow of life he couldn't find a more perfect partner for this than Della. First of all, she was a newcomer; she had seen nothing before in America and he easily surprised her with simple things. He could show her whatever he wanted in San Diego, and she would take it in with great appreciation. Della was like a happy child with wide-open eyes gazing rapturously at all the beauties of the city and nature. Herbert also felt like a newborn man. Again and again he invented new amusements for her, this 'naive poor refugee from Russia'.

Herbert had great pleasure taking Della out. He showered her with a cascade of invitations to restaurants, theaters, and concerts. Events followed in quick succession. Della was almost thirty years younger than his wife, very attractive, intelligent, could behave herself, and was able to talk about everything even with her limited English.

There was a specific "charm" that he was dating a Russian lady. He attracted everybody's attention and really enjoyed being in the center of it; it was something new and unusual in his life.

Della watched him. His gait became light-footed, quick and swift. He looked wide awake and spontaneous, a young rooster, whose wings were changed from dull to brightly colored, from tiredly wilting to quivering with fresh enthusiastic energy, prepared immediately to fly. Herbert was ready to sing cock-a-doodle-doo so loudly with a new youthful voice that it could be heard all the way to Russia.

Herbert eagerly introduced Della to people he barely knew and to his good acquaintances alike:

"My lady is from Russia. She is only a few months in America. Yes, she speaks English fluently. Yes, she is very smart. Oh, I am so lucky to meet her, she is my dear sweetheart. She is my charming gardener who makes my soul blossom!"

He experienced a keen sense of importance when he gained somebody's attention with Della. He was constantly being told:

"Where did you find such a beautiful lady? You are lucky to have her!"

Herbert virtually danced with excitement. His eyes shone, he tried to embrace Della, to touch her whenever he could to prove to the entire world that she belonged to him. His every movement was playful, his speech was full of humor, and he laughed at her every joke.

Did You Ever Have the Chance to Marry an American Multimillionaire?

Della liked him so much. It was a pleasure to watch how a serious, established elderly man turned into a young person, beaming with joy. A gleam of undisguised admiration came to his eyes when he looked at her.

She was so proud as a woman that she could inflame him; he was fired with love like a young man.

Yes, she was very proud of herself. Perhaps Herbert's delight, continuously expressed to Della, liberated and transformed her. She never felt so desirable with a man; it awoke a powerful stream inside of her. In her youth Della was entirely different. She never felt such intense feelings of appreciation for a man in her entire life.

Unconsciously, Della felt she opened unknown sluices in Herbert's soul. With all her feminine intuition she felt that she unlocked something innermost sacred in him. In his seventieth year, Herbert sensed a staggering waterfall of feelings that he never was given as a younger man. Della was a blessing for him. Maybe God sent Della to Herbert as a reward for his long devoted life with his old wife. He received an opportunity to feel young again. For Herbert, Della was a woman that he couldn't even imagine in his sweetest dream would be his. New love was grand!

CHAPTER 7

THEY LAUGHED LIKE children and felt connected forever. Herbert seemed to her such a witty, sharp-minded man with an incredible sense of humor. He exuded amazing happiness and was so glad to laugh after such a long depression.

They talked about everything. How did they make it with her limited English? Della still doesn't understand it, but she doesn't remember that the language ever was a problem. He was very patient with her pronunciation, never corrected or interrupted her, and always understood perfectly what she had said to him. There was no subject that they couldn't discuss. Because Herbert was smart and well educated, she was very interested to hear his opinion about many questions that life offered to her in a new country.

She never saw him reading a book. Nonetheless, he was competent in any field that they touched upon: history or psychology, customs in the country or astrology, feelings or religion, art or music, whatever. But his favorite subject was investment. Here he got on his high horse. In this area Della was absolutely blank. Della acknowledged his wisdom in everything that he did. He took her worries very sincerely and tried to help with all his heart. Her confidence in him rose; she trusted him and was open to him.

Herbert wanted Della to look great near him. He was not satisfied with her clothes that she brought from Russia. He took her to a store and searched each rack, choosing dresses for her and carrying armfuls of them to a fitting room where she waited for him. It was hard work to try on such a large amount of clothes. From everything that he used to bring she usually chose one or two dresses; she didn't like the rest.

Della said to him, "Please, let me choose the clothes myself." "No, I always bought dresses for my wife. She trusted me."

Did You Ever Have the Chance to Marry an American Multimillionaire?

"I trust you too, but you don't know me as well as you knew your wife; you don't know my taste."

"I know better what you need in America."

Della smiled inside and accepted the situation as it was. He was the boss. He paid money. Della must obey. Honestly speaking, she did not resist. He was full of desire to be in the role of magician, opening for his lovely Russian lady this fairyland named America. She let him do it. It was such a delight to watch an impressive person in love. He was ready to catch a star from the sky for Della.

Dear Herbert, you cannot imagine how great you looked in Della's eyes! Near you she felt herself like a Queen of the Universe!

CHAPTER 8

All their outings became an exciting game for Herbert. He felt like a wizard who lit a magic lantern in front of Della, the more so since she was very undemanding. He was in love and made an extraordinary effort, trying to entertain his darling Della.

When Herbert called to let her know that he planned to go somewhere exciting and asked her to be ready, she sensed she was supposed to prepare herself for a recurrent performance. She must be dressed up very well, with good makeup, and "wear" a happy smile and good mood on her face.

Her hair was supposed to have exactly the same color, "Lucy Red", like the movie actress Lucille Ball. Della never saw Lucy and didn't have any idea how she looked. Herbert took her to a beauty salon and ordered this special dye for her hair. She was curious how American beauticians would make her look like a famous actress, and permitted this experiment with her hair. Every time when a beautician dyed her hair, Herbert inspected it, glanced over it as if Della immediately must transform into Lucy in her new role. Della's hairstyle was supposed to be very special. The hair in front had to be high and every curl had to be done in a certain way.

Because they saw each other every day and any moment he could call and come, she knew she must be "in shape" twenty-four hours a day. This made her tense.

Della enjoyed swimming in the pool in her apartment building and after swimming her hair did not look the way he liked. Della felt guilty because of this, and she methodically tried to restore every curl on her head after swimming.

He paid so much attention to her hair that she started to feel a growing inner resistance. Her sense of humor couldn't help her and something inside of her revolted against this stupid pressure he put on her with her hairstyle. Somehow she felt as if he had made her a mannequin for his own show.

Did You Ever Have the Chance to Marry an American Multimillionaire?

She looked at herself in the mirror, hurriedly restoring her curls before he arrived, laughed, and asked her reflection in the mirror: "Who is brainless with these crazy red curls: you or him?"

She used to joke with him: "Am I an actress in your show? If you want a show, I can perform something for you."

She dressed up in funny clothes with a big hat and made small entertainment at home. He liked her humorous performances and laughed. She was so close to his inner wants; he had graduated from the university as a drama major and held the highest awards in this profession. In his youth he was a radio announcer, performed in plays, sang very well, and played the trumpet. He couldn't make big money with these jobs, so he changed his focus and grew up to be a serious businessman.

Herbert adored the taste and the power of an actor's transformation. He was teary eyed with joy when he heard Della singing Yiddish songs he loved. She asked him to sing with her; he always answered evasively. He had already become inert to explore himself and express himself anew.

"You sing wonderfully, Dellishka. I enjoy listening."

"Let us do it together."

"No, you do it better."

Was he ashamed? No, he was not a shy person. She asked him to play trumpet, but he never did.

Della liked how Herbert created for her his own term of affection. In Russian, Della's tender name sounds like Dellochka. Herbert couldn't pronounce it and changed it to Dellishka.

She named him also in Russian - Herbertchik, and he was happy like a child when she called him this. Intuitively Della felt that he didn't hear many terms of affection in his life and longed for caressing words. Della showered him with endearments. He deserved it; his soul was so open for tenderness.

Herbert loved Della's jokes. He continuously repeated to her:

"Dellishka, you have an incredible sense of humor!"

"I am from Odessa, Herbertchik. Odessa has always been a special place in the life of Jewish people residing in the territory of the former

Soviet Union. Plus, Odessa was the officially recognized capital of humor in USSR. The humor of Odessa residents is known all over the world."

Being near Della, this impressive man roared with laughter until the tears ran down his face. Herbert was so smart and inventive, they had great times together. Della bathed in his love. She was so glad to have a man like Herbert who took care of her, especially after the considerable turmoil she had undergone.

CHAPTER 9

WHAT IS OUR life? Do we direct it or does some invisible power put the events happening to us in its own, unpredictable direction? Are we always in control? We think we are. It doesn't matter how hard we try, we don't know what tomorrow will bring. Something happens. Whether we like it or not, we should act immediately, we must coordinate all collisions and participants right now; our reaction has to be quick and spontaneous. There are no rehearsals in our 'life play'. If we are unable to use previous experience or we don't have enough inner intuition, we make harmful mistakes.

The major theme in Della's new 'life play' in America was her relationship with Herbert.

Handicapped Aunt Rachel became a *Prima Donna* in the minor theme of Della's life.

Why did Della bring her aunt to San Diego? Because Rachel's brother, Della's uncle, lived here many years with his family. Really, where was Della supposed to go with a sick, helpless, handicapped old woman?

Back in Ukraine, Della and Uncle were very close. She liked his family. Their relationship was always friendly and well disposed. They kept up with each other for many years, actually, since Della's childhood. It was not only a family relationship, it was a good strong friendship, stable and reliable.

Thirteen years elapsed. Uncle enjoyed California, Della still lived in Odessa; they both changed. So it was completely upsetting and confusing to Della when her uncle and his family did not welcome Rachel and her to San Diego. Alas, it was definitely not a pleasant twist in her life and very, very painful.

Rachel rarely left the bedroom, but when she did, it was either to go to the bathroom or to go to the living room to watch TV. She didn't understand a word in English, but she liked to stare at the colorful pictures on the screen, and, with authority, criticize these crazy American movies. It was a small TV and it didn't work very well. Della wanted to change it, so she asked Herbert:

"I have $400 dollars. Can you please help me choose a nice TV for this amount of money?"

Herbert brought her to the store and she chose a TV according the money she had. Herbert showed her a much better TV with a bigger screen, but it was more expensive, about $600 plus.

"Do you like it better?"

"Yes, certainly. When I have more money, I will buy it, but now I can have only what I am able to afford."

Della gave him $400. "Please, buy the TV I chose. You will do it much faster than me. I would like to look at what else they have in the store."

He returned from the register and said that they would deliver the TV tomorrow directly to her apartment. The next day a gorgeous TV with a bigger screen arrived. She called Herbert.

"They sent me a big TV. Is this your work?"

"Yes, darling. I added $200 and bought the bigger one. Will you forgive me?"

"But I do not know when I can give you back these $200." "You do not need to. It is my gift to you."

"Oh, thank you soooo much, I am very grateful, Herbertchik."

Hebert insisted she and Rachel change their one-bedroom apartment for a two bedroom.

"Why do you need to sleep in the living room? It is not good for you, it is not good for us. We need privacy."

Did You Ever Have the Chance to Marry an American Multimillionaire?

As a real estate broker, he quickly found a gorgeous two-bedroom apartment with two bathrooms just across the street from his own home and moved Della with Rachel there. He also took Della to a few stores to choose furniture for the second bedroom. He bought her a gorgeous set of bedroom furniture, and a new sofa and armchair for the living room. Della was shocked with his lavishness. Herbert surprised her each day.

Certainly, Rachel was in the middle of all these fountains of Herbert's generosity. She saw the new clothing and shoes Della put on. He also bought comfortable clothes for Rachel. Their refrigerator was full of delicious food that Della could not afford to buy herself.

Della made tasty dinners and Herbert was their guest. He was very polite with Rachel during these evening dinners, and because Della was busy in the kitchen, Herbert gave plenty of attention to her aunt. Rachel bloomed.

CHAPTER 10

DELLA NEVER WAS bored with Herbert. They talked and laughed, laughed and talked. He was a good listener and he particularly wanted to know as much as possible about her life in the Soviet Union. Della told him how she met the first Americans in her life. Herbert laughed hysterically at her resourcefulness.

Because some years ago Herbert worked at the radio, he offered Della a project:

"The story is so cute. Let us write it down and I will try to find some way to put in on the radio."

They did it. Here is the story about Della's experience with Americans in Odessa.

The First Americans in Della's Life

It was the year 1990. The Cold War was over. The Soviet government desperately needed foreign currency and welcomed tourists, especially from America. Little by little, the Americans started to come. Their curiosity about mysterious Russia was much stronger than the fear of those unpredictable communists.

Della lived in Odessa, a beautiful resort on the Black Sea with a high level of culture. The Soviet Union started to fall apart; the country was in a mess. Gold disappeared from jeweler's stores.

Jews were once again allowed to emigrate; the rest of the citizens envied and hated them. They blamed the Jews for everything. The Jews were always the guilty ones.

Della seriously started to think about emigration and tried to find any avenue to meet some Americans and communicate with them.

There was an old prestigious International Hotel in Odessa named "The Red Hotel". Secured and protected, this hotel was only for foreigners, mostly American.

Did You Ever Have the Chance to Marry an American Multimillionaire?

For the average Odessa citizens, the Red Hotel was a no-no territory. They were not permitted to put their nose inside.

Americans, who visited Odessa and stayed at The Red Hotel, were unreachable. There was no way to meet them. But the Americans refused this isolation. They wanted to communicate with Odessa's people.

As it is said, if you seek, you will find.

Somehow Della was introduced to the director of the committee who organized the leisure time for the American groups in Odessa. Their program itinerary scheduled one evening with an Odessa family including a dinner at their home. It looked like a protest to the invisible wall that the Soviet security system had built around Americans. This dinner was a challenge to the Odessa tourist committee. They had to find a trustful family to put the Americans there for an entire evening and leave them alone.

The director courted her (or pretended doing this) perhaps waiting to see if he could safely introduce American tourists to her. He found that she was an excellent cook. Despite many suspicious looks cast her way, he finally decided that she would not shoot or bite the Americans.

He said:

"American tourists want to spend an evening with an Odessa family. Would you like to prepare a nice dinner and invite a couple of Americans to your place?"

All Della's family at that time was a handicapped 83-year-old Aunt Rachel who lived with her. Della laughed:

"Do you think they will be interested in meeting Rachel?"

"You will be great by yourself."

"I barely speak English," Della said.

"Don't worry, they have a translator."

"Okay, I will do it. Would you like to come as well?"

"No, no, they won't like any officials at the dinner. They want to feel free."

The American's itinerary provided 3 hours to dine with a Soviet family on Tuesday, from 6 to 9 p.m. When Della agreed to this adventure, the director informed her that he would be sending her not two, but six Americans plus a translator.

Della burst into laughter.

"Why are you laughing?" he asked.

"You made your job simpler. It would take a lot of your time to find another trustful Odessa family. It is easier for you to send a whole bunch of Americans to my place, isn't it?" Della teased him.

"You are too sharp," he laughed.

"Don't worry, I can handle it. I will greet all of them," Della assured him.

Della was permitted to invite some friends. The leisure program would pay for the dinner expenses.

"My God," she thought, "I have to put together a whole party."

The director called her: "Please serve the dinner with three crystals."

"What does that mean?" she asked.

"One crystal for water or juice, the second for wine, the third for vodka."

"What?" Della asked him. "No. You make these 'three crystals' at your fancy hotel.

I will do it more simply. It is my home and my rules. Okay?"

"Okay. You are the boss."

Della laughed. They are really crazy about Americans. Three crystals! Funny expression. It is nice to remember it.

Della's mind played ping-pong with the idea of making this dinner. She should prepare an outstanding dinner. She must show these Americans what it means to have dinner with a Russian family.

"Why Russian? No, I am not Russian. I am a Jew. I will prepare Jewish food. I will tell them that I am a Jew. Should I invite some of my friends? Yes, it would be a good idea. No, it wouldn't. Who needs to know that I expect guests from America? Personal contacts with Americans are not welcomed."

To have Americans at her home and not to tell anybody? To keep this secret? Impossible! Della wanted the entire world to know it!

Tuesday? Not a good day. Della worked and usually came back home at 6:30 p.m. To prepare the dinner a day or two before, on Sunday? No, the food must be fresh. She needed a day off on Tuesday.

Della's boss was also a Jew. All Soviet Jews secretly cherished an emigration dream. Her boss studied English, pretending that he needed it for his dissertation.

Did You Ever Have the Chance to Marry an American Multimillionaire?

In the morning Della came to his desk.

"May I invite you to my place for a dinner on Tuesday?" she asked.

He looked at her with surprise. They had never socialized before.

She explained:

"I will be having a group from America over for a dinner. Would you be interested?"

His eyes sparkled with interest.

"Yes, perhaps."

"You are welcome to come with your wife."

"I am sure she will be pleased." He looked at the calendar. "Oh, I cannot. Unfortunately, it is my daughter's birthday. But if you need, take Tuesday off. We will pay you for this day."

Great! This is what Della needed.

She invited a couple of her Jewish friends in order to share the Americans with them. It was September - the blessed time in Odessa. The market had all one wanted of fruits and vegetables. She bought the best, and started creating wonders in her kitchen. Her Aunt Rachel came to the kitchen with her crutches.

"What is going on here?" she asked.

"We will have special guests," Della replied.

"How many?"

"Seven."

"Why are they so special?"

"They are from America."

"I don't remember that you have American friends. Did you ever meet them before?"

"No."

"Are you crazy? Don't you know that all Americans are gangsters? Do you want to bring to our home seven bandits?"

"Who told you this rubbish?" Della asked her aunt.

"You work, work, work, you don't know what is going on in the world. I know. I watch TV. I read newspapers. You must immediately stop doing anything for them."

She yelled at Della, banging on the floor with her crutches.

"You are tired; go to the balcony and rest," Della told her.

"I am not tired!" Aunt raised her voice.

"Okay, your crutches are tired. You will break the floor. Go to the balcony! Relax. I will talk to you later."

"You don't listen to me! I categorically forbid you to open the door to these bandits. They are all bandits!" She pointed her finger into Della's face and left to the balcony loudly crying.

Della worked hard for a few hours. To the accompaniment of her aunt's crying, she prepared a great dinner. Rachel dramatically refused to eat lunch. She walked into her room and slammed the door. Near 6 p.m., Della asked her to change from her robe to a nice dress.

The aunt yelled:

"No! You are a stubborn donkey. I don't want to see you and your darned Americans!"

At 6 p.m. the guests arrived. Kind smiling faces. They introduced themselves.

Florence and Irwin Blickstein, from Boca Raton, Florida.

Adrian and Rosemary Pinto, from Norwich, Vermont.

Virginia Foote, from Tucson, Arizona.

Ida Fowler, from El Paso, Texas.

They were a part of a senior group of medical professionals. Delighted to come to Della's home, they looked in amazement at the table covered with a colorful abundance of food.

"How could you find so much food?" they asked. "The shelves at your stores are empty."

"In my refrigerator," Della joked.

They couldn't believe that she prepared everything herself.

She announced, "This is not a Russian home, it is a Jewish home. I am a Jew. I want you to enjoy Jewish food. I live with my old aunt, but she doesn't speak English and asked to excuse herself. She has decided to stay in her room."

Irwin said, "We are also Jews. Does she speak Yiddish?"

"Yes, she does."

"Can I talk to her?"

"I hope so."

Did You Ever Have the Chance to Marry an American Multimillionaire?

They came to Rachel's room. Irwin started to talk to her. Della left them alone. In a few minutes the aunt called Della:

"Where is my lipstick? I need my best blue dress. Give me the mirror! I will come to the dinner!"

Three hours flew by like three minutes. They laughed and talked, talked and laughed, and sang Jewish songs. They sang to Aunt Rachel "A Yiddisher Mama". Who cared that Della's English was poor?

At nine o'clock the bus driver knocked on the door.

"We must go. This is the best time we have had on this trip. We would like for you to come and join us at The Red Hotel tomorrow at lunchtime. We will be there and we will wait for you."

"I am not allowed to enter The Red Hotel," Della said.

"Don't worry. We will take care of it," they insisted.

The next day Della brought them a gift, a beautifully illustrated book about Odessa. Their meeting was short; their schedule was very tight. She left with her hands full of souvenirs.

Perhaps they expressed their excitement about the evening in Della's home to the tour administration. She was placed on top of the list as Odessa's family to greet Americans. Every two weeks a different group of Americans came to Odessa. Della made two more dinners and met another twelve Americans. Before each dinner the first thing in the morning Rachel took her seat at the kitchen table to prepare vegetables for her darling Americans. She was giving instructions to Della how to make the food more delicious. At dinner time, waiting impatiently for the guests, Rachel was dressed up an hour before the guests were supposed to come.

Soon America discontinued this program. It was not a pleasure for the tourists to see depressed people and empty store shelves.

In 1992 Della immigrated to America. She called some people who visited her home in Odessa. One couple from Seattle, Zelma and Erwin Kremen, came to San Diego to see Della in 1993. She was with Herbert already and he invited them to the best restaurant.

Florence and Irwin Blickstein often telephoned Della from Boca Raton, Florida. Irwin talked to Rachel for hours in Yiddish.

Nobody believed in 1992 that Rachel would survive the flight to America. But she lived in America for a long time.
Della's boss Eric Edelberg lives in New York now.
All American names in this story are real.

CHAPTER 11

Herbert did not have a chance to put this story on the radio. But it was the one that Della would eventually introduce to Americans by reading it on stage in a big theater, years later.

Herbert lived in the clouds. He was overflowing with love. He couldn't understand what was happening to him; he couldn't believe that he felt like a young man. He had never experienced these feelings in his entire life. Did it come from God? Herbert decided to talk about this with his rabbi whom he knew for many years. He even made a special appointment with the rabbi at his synagogue.

"I am 71. Is it possible to feel such strong love at my age? I love her like a teenager; I never felt like this even when I was young. I never loved my wife like this. I cannot imagine how this is possible."

"Yes, it is possible," the rabbi answered. "It is your great luck. It might be God's special blessing. Give your thanks to God for sending you this wonderful lady and these feelings at your age. You should feel yourself in Seventh Heaven."

When Herbert told Della about his visit to the rabbi, she was surprised.

"Why did you need a rabbi if you feel good?"

"Oh, he helped me. Now I really feel in Seventh Heaven."

"So, the rabbi approved of me, didn't he?" Della laughed.

Herbert was serious. His voice became firm.

"Do not laugh! I needed his explanation. For me you are the most important person in my life. I do not know how it happened, but it happened. I am repeating again and again: you are my charming gardener who makes my heart blossom."

Della came closer to him, hugged him, kissed his eyes, and whispered in his ears:

"Every day I thank God for you, Herbertchik."

"Dellishka, talk to me, please. You have such a wide life experience, do not hold it inside. Tell me everything related to your emigration," Herbert asked her again and again.

"It is too much. You will become tired of listening."

"Oh, no, what you are going to tell me, I will not read in any book or in any newspaper."

Della talked to Herbert, at the same time evaluating herself and her life. She trusted him and felt a strong need to share what she went through in her life. She kept too much inside being many years at the edge of depression. It became a release for her soul.

"Herbertchik, maybe I am telling you too much, but you are right, I need to talk it out. Hopefully it will help me with my insomnia. Sleepless nights are my problem now. Pills do not help me. I really want to forget about many things and never talk about them again, especially about my marriage. I must take everything negative out from my mind. It is my personal workshop with myself."

To her own surprise these talks helped her to understand that many things she went through in Odessa prepared her and led her to this new experience in America.

CHAPTER 12

THERE WERE ONLY a few months left before Della's departure to America. Almost no time left and so many things must be done. It seemed that the old life constantly pulled Della back, held her tightly and did not let go so she could jump into a new one. Thousands of new problems appeared every day. She rushed to deal with them and this exhausted her terribly. Only the day of departure could stop this fussing. But departure didn't look like a release for her. Its impending approach made her more depressed. It seemed to her that this process would never be over.

Whatever she did, wherever she went, the same persistent thought constantly flashed in the deepest level of her mind: *What are you doing, why are you rushing? You are wasting your time and strengths. The only thing that you must do is to study English. The rest doesn't matter and isn't worth a penny.*

Della constantly looked for any opportunity to hear real English.

When a new wave of emigration started in the USSR, self-styled teachers of the English language appeared in the city like mushrooms after a good rain. But their English was flooded with Russian pronunciation. Della cherished every chance to hear real, not Russian distorted, American English.

It was the beginning of the year 1992. Della already had her permission to go to America. Once, crossing Deribasovskaya Street, the main street of Odessa, she noticed a man standing in the middle of the sidewalk talking loudly in English and handing out fliers. The man had a lot of black hair and a big beard, very distinguished in the crowd. He was small and tiny, but his voice was so strong that he attracted everybody's attention.

Certainly, Della could not miss the possibility to catch an English conversation. She told this man a few English words. He looked tired from passing the fliers to indifferent people rushing by. He became animated when Della approached him. She dared to talk to this man with her limited English. Actually, he did not expect anybody to speak perfectly the language of Shakespeare in the middle of a Ukrainian city and was very glad to talk with Della. He said that he came to Odessa from Los Angeles as a missionary and introduced himself as a rabbi of a congregation called "Jews for Jesus." His name was Avi Snyder.

My God, a real American from California was in front of Della. She could speak with him, she could touch him. She wanted to ask him a thousand questions, but her tongue was frozen in her mouth, helplessly trying to find some appropriate English words. But she talked anyway, she did not want to give up. New English words appeared in Della's mind letting her continue this conversation.

The man told Della that he was going to give a number of lectures about a religious trend "Jews for Jesus" in the House of Science. Della knew this building very well. She did not care for the subject of the lecture; the most valuable part was the opportunity to hear real American English.

Della came home, laughing at herself how she dared to talk to an American man with only her few English words.

The next day she went to the House of Science. Rabbi Avi Snyder made a good presentation, attracting many people. The House of Science was overcrowded. Too many people were interested in fresh American news from the original source. They definitely were more interested to hear about America than about this particular religious trend.

The rabbi started his lecture. The interpreter helped him, but the translation was slow and unprofessional and the lecturer finally refused it. His speech was so powerful that the air in the auditorium seemed to be charged with electricity. People listened to him, holding their breath, and it didn't matter that they couldn't clearly understand him.

Rabbi Avi Snyder came from Los Angeles with an assistant, a woman who quietly walked among the audience helping to provide services and talking to people in Russian. Her name was Lisa. Lisa, a Jewish woman about Della's age, was a former immigrant from Leningrad.

Did You Ever Have the Chance to Marry an American Multimillionaire?

Della told Lisa that in a couple of months she was going to leave Odessa for good and hopefully would live in San Diego, California.

"Really? San Diego is just two and a half hours drive from Los Angeles, we will be neighbors. Let us meet and talk!" Lisa said.

Della invited her for dinner to her home and they became friends.

CHAPTER 13

It was 1992, a hard time in Ukraine. The Soviet Union fell apart. Ukraine fought for its separation from the Soviet Union and finally got it. Ukraine became independent, but was helplessly unprepared for this action.

Refusing Russian rubles, the Ukrainian government hurriedly issued new currency so fast, they even didn't have a name for it. They called it simply "coupons." The hustle-bustle with coupons was crazy.

In the beginning people paid a lot of Russian rubles for these so-called money-coupons. Everybody tried to get rid of rubles. Several weeks later the Ukrainian government printed so many coupons that they became as cheap as paper.

Rubles became a foreign currency. Now it belonged to another country named Russia and started to be fantastically expensive. People were so sorry that just a few weeks ago they stupidly lost so many rubles. Now everything became opposite: people paid a lot of coupons to get rubles back. The hustle with money was incredibly ridiculous. Provisions started to disappear from the stores.

Della tried to sell her furniture and belongings. Nobody wanted to buy anything at this crazy time, people did not have money. If she was lucky to find buyers, they paid coupons. What could she do with these coupons? It was forbidden to take much currency abroad. Only $200 per person was allowed. Additional dollars or other money could be confiscated during customs control.

The Ukrainian government showed its 'generosity'. They declared that they would pay pension for six months ahead to pensioners who emigrated. Why for six months, not for four or eight? There is no answer. They issued a rule: they paid the pension in coupons just a few days before departure. Why? Because the value of coupons changed every day, so they needed to pay people updated amounts of money. The real reason was that

Did You Ever Have the Chance to Marry an American Multimillionaire?

each day the coupons were worth less and less, which saved the government money.

Two days before her departure Della received a bagful of coupons. She knew that no other country accepted this new Ukrainian currency. She couldn't go to the bank and exchange them for dollars. The banks didn't have dollars. In fact, there was even a large sign on the bank door that said: *No exchange coupons for dollars.* It was practically impossible to change coupons in the bank for any currency, even to rubles. Della had no idea what to do with this huge bag of coupons, unless to give them away to friends in Odessa or to bring them to America for a souvenir.

In two days they were supposed to leave for Moscow and then to New York. In Moscow nobody needed Ukrainian currency. It seemed to Della that paying pensions with worthless coupons was the government's solution to get rid of these coupons that they foolishly printed in big amounts. Giving them to old people who gave their entire life to this country was an outrageous insult.

Della called Lisa asking for advice. Lisa immediately offered to exchange these coupons for dollars at the current rate. Della brought Lisa a big bag full of coupons, which represented Della's and Rachel's half-year pensions, plus the money for furniture Della sold at the last moment. At the current rate (180 coupons for one dollar) that entire bag was worth only $240. Della worked for 32 years as an engineer; her aunt worked for 35 years as an accountant. A half year of pension, $240 for both of these two professionals who worked their entire life in the Soviet Union, was a mockery. But at that time this amount of money was a fortune for Della.

Shortly after Lisa exchanged the Ukrainian coupons for dollars, Della and Rachel left for California. Lisa continued her mission in the Ukraine. Della lost track of her, but the gratitude to this woman warmed her heart for many years.

"Look, Herbertchick, what I have!"

Della showed him her "treasure collection" she brought from the falling apart Soviet Union.

"These coupons were first money that new independent Ukraine produced. It was real money. Now those coupons became souvenirs."

Herbert look at these coupons with curiosity.

"This currency disappeared already in Ukraine. For American collectors, who collect money from around the world, it could be a valuable addition."

Did You Ever Have the Chance to Marry an American Multimillionaire?

"And here are Russian rubles. This currency was valuable in 1991 and also disappeared forever from the market. As you can see below, the bills have a portrait of Lenin. It can be also a valuable addition to collectors.

"Herbertchick, let us have fun. I found something unique in my papers that I brought to America. Look at this so called 'document!'

It is a priceless treasure. This paper is a brilliant invention of the new born Ukrainian government which just declared its independence. It is written in Ukrainian (God forbid Russian!) to declare to everybody that, yes! Ukrainian language definitely exists! It is grocery coupons. Because the shelves in our stores were empty, the government created these coupons for employed people who were busy with their jobs and were not able to stay in long lines. I received it each month at my design office. This particular one was for September.

"It was supposed to have a stamp. Without a stamp it was not valid. With this paper I could buy a limited amount of groceries such as flour, groats and so on, but not sugar."

"What was wrong with sugar?" Herbert laughed.

"Oh, sugar was such an important product. To buy sugar they created a special 'invitation.' Look at this small shred of paper. It has a sign:

Invitation
to buy
S u g a r
November
Valid
till November 30
City Odessa
1991 y.

Did You Ever Have the Chance to Marry an American Multimillionaire?

"This 'invitation' allowed me to buy one kilogram of sugar per a month for the family. This shred of paper also was valid only with a special stamp on the back. I was on a business trip, couldn't use it before November 30 and came to the store in the beginning of December. No, they did not give sugar to me. Luckily, I received already the December's 'invitation' and got the desired kilogram of sugar. This one for November appeared to be between my papers and accidentally I brought it to America. Now it looks like a funny souvenir."

Herbert laughed.

"You are laughing, Herbertchik, living here, in America. We did not laugh in 1991 in Odessa. By the way, this 'document' is more than quarter of century old. Maybe it should belong to a Museum.

"People who did not have jobs couldn't have these coupons and 'invitations.' They had a really difficult time buying food."

"It was a crazy time," Harold said.

"Oh, really crazy. But at this time I was awarded with a Medal. In the Soviet Union the age of retirement was different than in the USA: women could retire at the age of 55, men at the age of 65. I took this chance, made my retirement at 55 in 1990. As an award, they gave me this medal.

"I was retired, but did not leave my design office. I continued to work, receiving my pension and salary. I made my preparations for immigration and needed money. It helped a bit. By the way, it is the only medal my country gave to me. What should I do with this piece of metal now?"

"Just keep it!" Herbert said.

"What for?" Della shook her shoulders.

"It is your life, Dellishka!"

CHAPTER 14

Let us look *a little bit forward. About twelve or more years elapsed. Della lived in San Diego. There is a widely famous health institution here: Optimum Health Institute. People from different cities and countries come here for detoxification and other health purposes. Della also decided to have a retreat there.*

Sitting in their dining room, she noticed two women, mother and daughter, who cheerfully talked in Russian. Russian? Here, in this place? Being curious, Della told them something in Russian, and the three of them started to talk in their native tongue. Mother lived in New York, her name was Elizabeth, and her daughter Lana was from Los Angeles. They decided to meet here, in San Diego.

"I am from San Diego, I live not so far. You are welcome to be my guests," Della said.

"Where are you from originally?" Elisabeth asked Della, curious about her accent.

"Odessa, Ukraine."

"Odessa? I know Odessa very well. I worked there as a missionary for two years in the most crazy time when the Soviet Union was falling apart. 1991 to 1992. A very tough two years."

Della looked again at the woman. A missionary? 1992? Not too many American missionaries were in Odessa at that time. That was the year when Della made preparations for immigration and searched for each connection with America. She looked attentively at Elizabeth. No, she did not recognize her. But the name... Elizabeth... Elizabeth? Lisa? No, no! It was impossible. Impossible?

Suddenly Della asked Elizabeth: "Jews for Jesus? The House of Science?"

The expression on Elizabeth's face and widely opened eyes said it all!

"What? How do you know about Jews for Jesus and The House of Science? Have you been there? In 1992?"

Nothing is impossible... Yes, it was Lisa.

"Lisa, Lisochka, don't you recognize me? I cannot believe that it is you."

She looked at Della.

51

"I am so sorry. There were so many people around me, it's hard to remember."

"I did not recognize you either. You helped me tremendously in Odessa. Remember, you changed those idiotic coupons for dollars for me. I was so touched and grateful," Della said.

"I did it many times for people. I needed to change my dollars for coupons anyway to pay for rent, food and so on. So I was glad to help you."

"Thank you. It was a tremendous help at that time. You were at my house in Odessa, remember? I wanted to call you when I came to America, but I did not have any contact telephone number."

"Oh, my God, yes! Now I remember. You left too fast."

"Yes, before departure you exchanged my big bag of coupons for dollars. You gave me 240 dollars! Two hundred forty dollars! I never had so many dollars in my life! I felt like a millionaire with this amount of money. I was afraid to take this fortune through the custom control and so I hid it in a coffee can under the coffee. Yes, we left two days later. You couldn't give me any telephone in Los Angeles, you did not have it, you lived in Odessa at that time."

∽∽∽

Lisa now lives in New York City and continues to help people. Here, in America, she is Elizabeth Terini.

The wheel of fortune connected Della to Lisa in Odessa when Della desperately needed her help. And then the wheel of fortune brought Lisa into Della's life again years later, in America. Unpredictable twists of life. Again and again Della learned: unpredictable twists of life are not accidental. They are meant to be.

CHAPTER 15

Now, WHEN DELLA describes her life story, she starts to really believe that many things in her life had happened for a reason. That meeting with American Rabbi Avi Snyder from Los Angeles on the Deribasovskaya Street in Odessa brought Della not only Lisa, but also wonderful friends in San Diego.

Back in Odessa, Rabbi Snyder gave Della a referral letter to Rabbi Barney Kasdan who lived in San Diego. Della called Rabbi Kasdan. He gladly welcomed Della and invited her for a dinner in his house. It was such a warm meeting. Della's English was poor, but it did not matter, they communicated perfectly.

Della came to their synagogue. It was a powerful, wonderful service, in both English and Hebrew. Hebrew made it somewhat complicated for Della. Later she was invited to a great Thanksgiving party in the synagogue. There she met Barbara, Jan, and their cute five-year-old little Sylvia. Della dared to sing Russian songs such as "Moscow Nights" and "Dark Eyes", while Barbara, who knew these songs, accompanied Della on the piano.

Did we forget about Herbert in this deviation from the main subject? We did not. Just Della tried to establish connections with other people in San Diego, and many whom she met at that time became her lifetime friends. Barbara and Jan were among them.

The first Thanksgiving in America. Herbert was invited to a family reunion in Los Angeles for this holiday. He had only known Della for just a few weeks and it was not appropriate yet to bring her to this family event.

Fortunately, Barbara and Jan invited Della to share Thanksgiving with them. They lived far away from Della, but Jan drove a long way to take her to their house. Della appreciated the warm, welcoming atmosphere of their home, and the beautiful spread of delicious food with a huge stuffed turkey, the 'queen', on the table. Barbara and Jan became an important part of Della's life for many years ahead. Little Sylvia grew up and became a gorgeous young woman.

People come together. We attract each other. How can we recognize when the right people cross our path? On what level does this connection happen? Sometimes it seems like the Unknown Director from Beyond orchestrates particular situations in our life. Neither Della nor Barbara and Jan could have ever guessed that the seeds of their close relationship had been planted way back on Deribasovskaya Street in Odessa, Ukraine, where in 1992 Della dared to converse with Rabbi Snyder in her broken English.

CHAPTER 16

"How did you come to the United states?" Herbert continuously asked Della.

"By a miracle, Herbertchik, by a miracle."

"What do you mean 'by a miracle'? Can you tell me about this miracle, please, Dellishka?"

"It is too long a story, Hebertchik."

"That's okay, I am willing to hear this."

"Well, I like the idea about writing down the story, like you did with the previous story. But my English is not so good," Della said.

"I will help you. You do your best. And I will edit it."

"Promise?"

"Of course!"

For your enjoyment, dear reader, below there is the next story about Della's way to America.

America? Just a Joke . . .

At the beginning of February, 1991, my dear friend Fiana invited me for a cup of tea. No, it was not in America. We still lived in the USSR, in our native city of Odessa, on the Black Sea.

It was the last evening before Fiana's thrilling journey to New York. Walking in the street and fighting a heavy snowfall, I anticipated the pleasure of our meeting.

My wonderful Fiana. We had met each other at the university when we were seventeen. Now, almost forty years later, as mature women, we still valued our friendship.

Shaking snow off my fur hat and coat, I knocked at her door.

"Hello, my American lady!" I hugged her.

"Not yet! Don't rush! Hold your horses!"

"*Okay, okay. You are my almost American lady!*"

She introduced me to another woman who was sitting at the table. The three of us sipped aromatic tea and enjoyed delicious food. Visiting America was really an exciting adventure; joy reigned at the table. Isolated from the entire world by the Soviet Iron Curtain, we knew so little about distant, powerful and enigmatic America. Our fantasies flowed freely.

Gorbachev had slightly opened this Iron Curtain. Tomorrow, one of us, Fiana, would make a huge leap into the gap in the impenetrable wall around the Soviet Union. Next morning she would fly into a different world, another dimension.

I watched Fiana. Is this our goodbye tea? Will she come back? Oh, yes, sure she will. There is no doubt. Her son and grandchildren are still here, in Odessa; she only has a visitor's visa. She cannot stay in the United States long. No, no! It is stupid to come back! She is not a fool. Will I ever see her again?

I couldn't ask Fiana this question. She didn't know the answer herself. It was a chaotic time in the Soviet Union; everything was falling apart. We didn't have the slightest idea what the near future would bring. We laughed, but our eyes, including Fiana's, expressed our worries and uncertainties. The United States had pressured the Soviet government to allow Jews to emigrate. Several countries had flung the door wide open for Soviet Jews, especially Israel. We, Soviet Jews, tried to find the most reasonable and secure way to get out of the Soviet Union. Certainly we did it secretly because we could lose our jobs. It was better not to ask too many questions.

The clock showed 11p.m. Our meeting was over. I said goodbye, then hugged and kissed Fiana. At the door she joked:

"*Oh, if you have the American applications, I will send them to Washington from New York!*"

"*Dreams, dreams, useless dreams!*" *Whispering this in her ear, I kissed her again and left.*

It was a beautiful, frosty night. The snow had stopped. A full, bright moon shone in a clear sky, a fresh carpet of snow glittered with myriads of diamonds. A night

Did You Ever Have the Chance to Marry an American Multimillionaire?

like this was so rare in Odessa; our sunny city doesn't have much snow in wintertime. My lungs welcomed the fresh air; it was so peaceful and quiet. Only the crunch of snow under my shoes disturbed the night's serenity.

I lived a twenty-minute walk from Fiana. I walked, watching this beauty, but the thoughts in my head danced their own dance, and I couldn't stop them.

American applications . . . The American government had established a special immigration-processing center in Washington. This center accepted applications from every Soviet Jew who wanted to immigrate to America. Applicants were put on a long waiting list. Those, who had close relatives in the United States, such as children or parents, brothers or sisters, had preference in getting permission to come to America. Cousins, uncles, aunts, etc. didn't count as close relatives.

Anyway, to be on this waiting list gave some hope. It would be a good idea for me to send the application to this processing center. American applications were available only at the American Embassy in Moscow. We could get them in Odessa too, but for a lot of money.

What is the matter with you? What is the difference: more money, less money? How can you get these applications now, in the middle of the night? Forget it and admire the fresh sparkling snow!

At that period of my life, emigration was a most painful problem. I had a big burden on my shoulders: an eighty-two-year-old, handicapped Aunt Rachel. Ten years before she fell and broke her hip. She had several surgeries, but the hip was never healed. She was unable to walk or to live by herself. An old maid, she never had any children.

I loved Rachel. At the time she broke her hip, I was also recovering from a recent serious surgery. Nevertheless, I took her to my apartment. She lived with me for ten long years and I cared for her all that time. It was impossible to leave her alone in the USSR.

My children, (my daughter and her husband) also had a hard time. The in-laws were divorced and the mothe- in-law recently had left for Israel. My ex-husband had left for the United States. The children had two choices: Israel or America. They decided to go to America. I could join them and immigrate with them, but Rachel, as an aunt, was an indirect relative and not eligible to go with us. She needed to be sponsored by a relative closer to her.

Rachel's brother had lived in California for a long time and had a large family. He refused to give Rachel an affidavit concerning their relationship, even though we were very close with him back in Odessa.

I walked; my feet sank in the soft snow. During this twenty-minute walk, my entire life flashed through my mind. The reality was too sad for me; I didn't have another choice except to surrender to it.

Because of Rachel, I cannot emigrate. Why do I need these applications? Forget it! No! Do I want to bury myself with an old handicapped aunt in the failing Soviet Union? Noooo!!! I need these applications! They might be the first step on my way to America. I must find a solution. I must get out of this prison and take my aunt with me! Where can I find those damn applications now?

Being absolutely nonreligious, but too frustrated, I looked up at the sky . . .

"God, dear God! I am so helpless and powerless; I cannot do anything on my own! Please, be with me, please, hear me. Help! Please . . ."

I walked, looking at the cold, clear sky with its stars. My feet slid on the ice hidden under fluffy snow. The windows were dark. People slept.

"Where are you, God?" Exhausted and hopeless, I approached my apartment. Abruptly I stopped, rooted to the ground.

"I do have the applications!!! I couldn't throw them away!!! I have them! They are somewhere in my home!!!"

Two years before my friend had brought me two American applications.

"I am going to Israel. I don't need them anymore. Keep them just in case. Who knows, they might be useful to you," he said.

I ran into my apartment, threw down my coat and boots, and rushed to the drawers where I kept all my papers. Chucking all contents from the drawers onto the floor, I looked thoroughly, but couldn't find the applications. I searched my bedroom. Nothing.

I came to Rachel's room, turned on the light.

"What happened?" she asked.

"Don't talk to me now, sleep!" I ordered.

Did You Ever Have the Chance to Marry an American Multimillionaire?

The apartment became a mess of papers, but I didn't see the applications. I became angry with myself.

Calm down and look through the papers again! Look under furniture and behind it! Take the drawers out!

There they were! I found the papers! I did! I couldn't believe it! Something impossible had happened, a miracle! Two American applications, for Rachel and me, were in my hands, in front of my eyes. I held them!

They were thick. I needed to answer hundreds of questions and to describe our background fully. It was two o'clock in the morning. Who cared? In my kitchen, I made a big pot of hot tea, put a warm shawl on my shoulders, took the pen, and started to answer all the questions.

At 7:00 a.m. I called Fiana: "I will come in twenty minutes! Wait for me, don't leave!" and hung up.

Not having a car, I ran. The snow was melting. Splashing through the water and mud, my boots slid on the slippery road. I didn't care. I rushed. I came to Fiana's apartment on the eighth floor and rang her doorbell.

"What happened?" her face looked frightened.

"Here are two applications for me and Rachel. Take them to my relatives in New York. Their names are Zhenya and Sam. Here is their telephone number and address. If they want to, they will help. Try. Listen to me carefully now! Don't dare come back! Do you hear me? Don't come back! Your son will find his way to America! And God help you, my love!"

Exhausted, I went home and took a shower, trying to get a bit of energy. I arrived at my job late and could hardly move a finger. But I felt that I had started something tremendously important in my life.

Fiana flew to New York. Several days later Zhenya and Sam came to her and she gave my applications to them.

"I will try my best! Tomorrow I will call Washington," Zhenya told Fiana.

Washington sent Zhenya a package with detailed instructions, asking her to fill out an affidavit about our relationship. She put the two thick applications in a big envelope, added her affidavit and sent it to the Washington Processing Center.

The first brick in the foundation was laid. In March, 1991 the clock started ticking.

◦◦◦

Two weeks later Zhenya called Washington to see if the package had arrived. They promised to inform her by mail within a week. Time passed without any reply from Washington. Zhenya called them, and again they asked her to wait. Several weeks later, the Washington center informed Zhenya with apologies that they had lost the applications and asked her to reapply. Two blank applications were enclosed in the envelope.

Having no clue about our personal information, Zhenya called Rachel's brother in San Diego. He was curious why a distant relative would ask him questions about his sister and was reluctant to give the information. Zhenya tried her best to explain to my uncle that it would be a good deed (a Mitzvah) to get us out of the Soviet Union and asked him to help her complete the forms. She filled out two new applications and sent them back to Washington. In early May, the Washington Processing Center notified Zhenya that they had accepted the applications.

About two weeks later, my children received a letter from Washington with a computer number for their case. Washington also informed them that on August 22, 1991 they must come for an interview to the American Embassy in Moscow. Any delay of this date could mean an additional year of waiting.

There was no doubt that the children must be in Moscow on time, no matter the situation with Rachel and me. Our position was hazy and theirs was clear. They had only three months to prepare the necessary papers which must be signed and notarized according to the Soviet law of emigration. To go through thousands of formalities and long lines in three months was a daunting task.

Unable to change anything in my situation, sick and tired, I gave up. I knew that processing the papers in Washington usually took over two years. I knew it would be impossible for me to emigrate with an old handicapped woman. I wouldn't be able to do it by myself. I also knew that I would never desert Rachel.

It is my fate. I must accept the situation as it is. My children will go away, I will live in Odessa forever in a failing country, missing my children and spending

Did You Ever Have the Chance to Marry an American Multimillionaire?

dreary days and nights near an old aunt. My life doesn't belong to me. It belongs to my old aunt. No! No! Nooooo! I don't want it! I must find a way out.

How? I had no clue.

My neighbor Zhanna, who was also my coworker, was making her own preparations for emigration. We shared the news with each other.

"How is your case moving?" she asked me.

"There is no hope for me. My children received the invitation to Moscow for an interview."

"Really? It means that they are already in the computer. Do you know their computer number?"

"Yes, I do. So what?"

"It is crucially important. What are you waiting for? Washington can coordinate your case with your children. Call your relatives in New York immediately."

∞∞∞

How did we call America in 1991? It was a special adventure. Phone calls had to be ordered in advance. If we placed an order today, we would be able to talk tomorrow. To make it happen we must dial "07," International Service, which accepted orders from 9 a.m. to 1 p.m. This number was always busy, so people spent hours dialing "07" without any result.

The next morning, I bravely made my stand near the telephone that kept shouting busy beeps in my ear. Without interruption, I dialed 0 and 7. My finger didn't stop for a moment. Finally, persistence was rewarded; I broke through, ordered the conversation, and the next day talked with Zhenya. She was not enthusiastic.

"There is no time left. I am not sure if it is possible, but I will try. I will call Washington," Zhenya said.

It was the middle of June already; I had no news from America. Fiana's son, who was still in Odessa, called me: "I talked with New York. Mama said that everything is fine with your papers. Washington accepted them."

I thanked him for the good news, but nothing was clear to me. What did "accepted" mean? Did they put my papers into a general waiting list or did they join my papers with my children case? I had no idea, but didn't feel comfortable about bothering Zhenya again.

In the meantime, almost every day one of my dear friends emigrated and called me to say "Good bye." Emptiness in my life increased. How sad to feel this growing vacuum around and to wave "Good bye" to friends. I told them "See you." Will I? One of my dear friends, Luba, was going to New York shortly. I asked her to call Washington as soon as she arrived in America.

"Why do you need me to call?" she asked. "You can call yourself. Here is the telephone number of the Washington Processing Center."

"But I cannot speak English!"

"You don't need to!" she retorted."They have a Russian department."

From then on, I could handle the situation myself. Again I endlessly dialed "07." Again I succeeded and the next day talked directly to the Washington Center. A man answered:

"You don't have a computer identification number yet. I can try to ask permission to join you to your children, but I am not sure about your aunt."

"She is old and handicapped, she cannot live by herself."

"I understand. But we have certain rules about relationships. It could be an obstacle. Does she live with you?"

"Yes."

He looked at the computer.

"I see. She has the same address. It might help. I cannot tell you anything now. I will write a letter about your situation to my supervisor. Please, call in two weeks."

"What are our chances?"

"Fifty-fifty. But I will try my best." I thanked him and hung up.

July began. I called Washington again. The same man came to the telephone.

"My congratulations. You are both on the list. You and your aunt. You have a computer number. Here it is, write it down. When your children live in America

Did You Ever Have the Chance to Marry an American Multimillionaire?

for two years, they will be able to send you an invitation with an affidavit about your relationship and you will be able to come to the United States."

"No, I will not. I cannot do it alone, especially with an old handicapped woman. It would be impossible for me to emigrate, handling my aunt by myself. No, if the children leave without us, it means that I will never emigrate. Can you, please, try to join us to the computer number of my children due to these circumstances?"

"I am not sure that it is possible. Two people: mother and aunt. I need to talk to my supervisor. Can you wait, please?"

"I will."

In a moment or so, this man would tell me Washington's decision that could change my life completely. Every muscle in my body was tense, waiting for his verdict: life or death. Impatiently sitting in the chair with the telephone at my ear, I tried with utmost effort to calm myself. Again I prayed to God, repeating like a mantra: "Help me, God, help, please, help."

Holding the telephone a minute, two, five, ten . . . I listened. . . there was no sound. I reset it. It didn't give any echo, any squawk. My telephone was disconnected, dead. It had never happened before. Did I pull out the plug accidentally? No, everything looked fine. I tapped the telephone, knocked it, yelled into it — nothing. I was ready to break this machine that failed so shamelessly at the most important moment in my life.

Neighbors? Our telephones were on a party line. Maybe they had talked? No, it was impossible. If I was talking, they could not. The neighbors were Zhanna's family; they knew how important the conversation with Washington was. They lived two floors above me. I ran up the stairs.

"Something is wrong with my telephone. Is yours okay?" I asked. They lifted it. "It sounds normal."

I grabbed their telephone and listened. Nothing wrong.

"Did you talk recently?"

"No, we didn't."

"Please, don't touch it for a half hour. I was talking to Washington and was somehow disconnected. I must finish this conversation."

"Okay."

I ran downstairs to my apartment. My telephone was still dead. Like a wounded animal in a cage, I flung myself about the room trying to understand what had happened. Finally, forty-five minutes later (!), my telephone became alive again. I called the International Service, asking to connect me back to Washington.

"I cannot do it now. We have only two hours communication time with America and it is over," a woman – the operator—explained.

"Something was wrong with my telephone line and it is not my fault. This conversation is vital for me. Please, reconnect me. Please, do whatever you can. I promise, I will send you a special gift. Please, try."

"Yes, I heard your conversation with Washington. They put you on hold. I cannot promise, but I will try my best."

She did it! She connected me to Washington! An American woman, speaking Russian with a heavy accent, asked me to whom I would like to direct my call.

"I spoke with a man an hour ago. I cannot tell you his name."

"Did he speak Russian with an accent?"

"No, he spoke very well."

"I will try to find him. Wait, please."

Wait . . . Again . . . I looked nervously at the telephone, holding it like a crystal ball. I was afraid something would happen again.

"I tried to reach you. You disappeared," the same man said to me. "There is very good news for you. Your request was accepted. You and your aunt have permission to emigrate with your daughter. You can come together with them for the interview at the American Embassy in Moscow on August 22."

"What? We can go together with my daughter for the interview?"

"Yes, you can. You must. You have been accepted."

Good news can be as stressful as bad. All the tension and pressure of the last several months blew up inside of me. I lost control of myself and . . . burst into hysterical sobs. It was like a volcanic eruption. My body refused to hold onto my emotions. I could not stop this explosion and sobbed loudly into the telephone.

"Please, don't cry. Everything is fine. You will come to America. You will live here. Please, believe me. I swear to you, you will. Please, dear Dellochka, don't cry! Please . . . I am telling you, you are fine, Dellochka, please . . ."

Did You Ever Have the Chance to Marry an American Multimillionaire?

"There is no time left. I don't know how to make it. I have no proof, no invitation, they won't even let me enter the Embassy," I sobbed.

"The American Embassy will have all the information."

"I need to do tons of paper work, to fill out all the forms. I have nothing." I wept.

"Your children received the papers from us. Make copies from them and put your information on the copies."

"The Soviet authorities won't sign any form without official papers from America in my name."

"I will mail the package to you immediately, right now."

"It takes a whole month or more to get the mail from America," I panicked.

"You will receive it on time, trust me. Now go to the mirror, wipe your tears and sing the happiest song you know, okay?"

I cried.

"Please, don't cry, give me a good smile. Never cry anymore. Promise?" he talked to me as if I were a baby . . .

"Yes . . .." I whispered through tears.

"See you in America."

My dear man, I didn't even ask your name. Please, forgive me. I think I didn't remember my own name at that moment. Thank you for your consoling, encouraging words. The sympathy and support you sent me from Washington, your kindness that flew to me from another continent across the Atlantic Ocean, through half of the world, I will remember forever.

I sent a gift to the woman who connected me to Washington when time was up. I also paid a fortune for this telephone conversation. It was the best investment I ever made.

∽⌒∽

Exhausted and in tears, I came to Rachel's bedroom and sat on her bed.

"We're going to America." I whispered.

"Together?"

"Yes, I got permission for you. I will take you with me. You will see your brother!"

I looked at my aunt, at her crutches. She will accompany me to my new American life. It was not promising to come with an old helpless woman to a new country. How was I to get her to the United States?

Don't think about this now! You succeeded in getting permission for Rachel! This is most important. You won't leave her alone. You will bring her to her brother. He has a big family. You won't need to carry this huge burden alone anymore. You will breathe! You will finally live your own life!

I had hope! I felt fresh air. At that time I didn't realize how tremendously difficult this journey would be. I was too naive.

There was only a month left before the interview in Moscow. My children were busy with their own things. My head boiled. First, I must prepare all the papers and get hundreds of signatures from Soviet officials. I must start the conveyor with the papers immediately. So many copies, for me, for Rachel, and endless lines at endless offices. I never knew of their existence before. Now they showed up in our huge bureaucratic machine. A torrent of unpredictable details needed immediate attention every day.

All family members were required to come to the American Embassy for a medical examination, no exceptions. The Embassy had only one reason: if a person was unable to come to Moscow, it meant he or she would be unable to go to America. That is all. How could I get Rachel to Moscow? She hadn't left the apartment for several years.

A wheelchair. Yes, she needed a wheelchair. Where to get it? It wasn't easy to find one in Odessa. I made endless calls, additional appointments at many offices, waited in lines to get the required signatures. Finally I got a wheelchair for Rachel.

I needed to ask doctors to prepare her for this trip, so I invited several doctors to visit Rachel and watch her. Every week they prescribed new medicines that kept me running to pharmacies. The number of pills she must take per day increased to twenty-seven.

I told the doctors: "It is too much for an 82-year-old woman. How can she take so many chemicals?"

Did You Ever Have the Chance to Marry an American Multimillionaire?

"She needs all of them" they told me. "Tell her to take them separately."

I hate pills myself and always have a pharmaceutical reference book in my home. I read all Rachel's prescriptions carefully, especially about their side effects. After this investigation, I asked Rachel to skip some of the pills. But Rachel, being a disciplined woman, took all the pills according to the doctors' orders. Several days later, I heard a sound in the corridor. I ran there and found Rachel on the floor, unconscious. Walking to the bathroom, she had fallen. Thank God, I was home. I called emergency. Emergency recognized a medicine poisoning. They made Rachel regurgitate. This saved her.

❧

How could I manage all these worries, endless lines, care for Rachel, and do my full time work as an engineer-designer in the movie industry? Now it is a big puzzle for me. Perhaps, if we have a goal, our resources are infinite.

Finally, all papers were prepared. The last step was to notarize them. In such a huge city as Odessa, only one law office notarized emigration documents. At that time, thousands of people emigrated; they had to stay in the line almost all night to enter the office in the morning. This law office had a strict rule: only people with an official invitation from the United States could have their documents notarized. The package from Washington for Rachel and me hadn't come yet. There was no more time to wait.

I was crushed. All the worries, efforts, conversations with Washington, sleepless nights—everything seemed in vain and stupid. The papers won't be signed, my children would depart to America, and I would stay with Rachel in Odessa.

God, dear God, for what sins did you reward me with such a destiny?

Searing back pain put me flat in bed. Every muscle moaned; my body and mind, crushed by excruciating grief, failed to obey me. Helpless, hopeless, worn-out, I was even unable to cry.

My daughter and her husband shared the turns. He arrived at this law office at 3 a.m. at night. My daughter took his post at 8 a.m. in the morning. She must leave at 1 pm. There was still a need to stay in line. So the other rushed from home to take the place in the line. Just in case, he checked the mailbox. A *package from Washington with the official invitation and papers for Rachel and me waited in their mailbox. All our documents were notarized. With this news the pain in my back dissolved.*

God, dear God, was it your will?

⁂

We had airline tickets to Moscow for August 20, 1991 in order to come to the American Embassy on August 22. On August 19 all radio stations, TV and newspapers exploded with reports about a government coup in the Soviet Union. On the night of August 18, 1991, outside of the ruling power and the law, President Mikhail Gorbachev was removed. No reasons were given to justify this. Tanks took up positions on all the bridges in central Moscow. A state of emergency had been declared and troops had been brought in to keep order. Nobody knew exactly what had happened in Moscow. Contradictory statements, conflicting surmises, endless questions, danger warnings—all poured out from the radio and TV, assaulting our brains. Was it the start of a civil war? We had no idea. We knew only that it didn't matter what was going on in Moscow; we still had to go there.

We couldn't. Moscow was closed. No planes were flying to Moscow until further notice. Nor were trains running. On August 20, the second day of the coup, we ventured to Odessa's airport. Rachel, in the wheelchair, led our parade. We showed our tickets and all our papers, explaining the urgency of being in Moscow on time. "Wait . . ." they told us. How long? Nobody knew.

The first airplane that was allowed to fly to Moscow took us on board. Did we fly to the epicenter of the war? We heard the first reports of shots fired and troops and tanks concentrated in Moscow. The airplane's radio informed us continuously. We knew that demonstrators had erected barricades around the White House in Moscow, using trash trucks, concrete blocks, benches, and trees.

(The White House in Moscow? Yes, in Moscow. It is a beautiful huge building where the highest Russian government offices are located.)

Concrete barriers were constructed on the main roads to prevent tanks from approaching the White House. Moscow hospitals were preparing to receive the wounded, particularly tear-gas injuries. People around the White House were

Did You Ever Have the Chance to Marry an American Multimillionaire?

advised to carry wet handkerchiefs with which to cover their noses and mouths in case of a gas attack. A mobile medical treatment center was established. The defenders had at their disposal automatic weapons and bottles of homemade incendiary liquid, boxes of which were standing near.

(An interesting note: my editor, trying to give a better expression, crossed homemade incendiary liquid and put above Molotov cocktails. This is an American expression. I did know in Russia that Americans named these bottles Molotov cocktails.)

Overwhelmed with this awful information, we arrived in Moscow. All highways were blocked. Instead of the usual forty-five minutes, we drove from the airport four hours through Moscow's suburbs to our relatives where we had arranged to stay.

Our appointment in the American Embassy was scheduled at 11 a.m. on August 22. We didn't know if it was open or closed. On August 21, all day long we called the Embassy with no result. In the early morning of August 22 we arrived at the American Embassy. Many people were already standing in a long, fenced in line along the building and there we took our place. American guards and Russian militia patrolled us. The American Embassy was located not far from the White House. It was a beautiful summer morning, but the atmosphere was oppressive.

An armed military unit marched in the direction of the White House. Demonstrators appeared with their slogans. Military cars passed by. After three hours of waiting, we finally entered the Embassy. Security procedures took a great deal of time. Then we waited inside. When we finally came to the registration window, showing our papers, a deafening siren rang out inside the American Embassy. In minutes the entire building was empty; we found ourselves on the street.

Security forces checked the building and allowed people to reenter. Again the same thorough security control, interminable waiting inside, and checking of papers. The interview with the American representative was short. After several formalities he asked:

"Why do you want to emigrate?"

"Because as a Jew I face endless obvious and invisible obstacles here. It is impossible to fight them. It affects every area of our life, above all, health and career."

"For example?"

"My mother couldn't move well after a stroke and broke her hip. I put her in the hospital and paid all the nurses to keep an eye on her. One night a new nurse came. Turning my mother in bed, this nurse grabbed her broken hip and literally wrenched the leg. My mother died, after suffering unbearable pain. I don't want to go through this myself."

The American representative looked at me with sympathy. There were no more questions.

The interview was over. We must come back to the Embassy at 6 p.m. to get the decision. Since we had several hours to wander around, we walked as far as we could in the direction of the White House. A trolleybus, turned upside down, with a crumpled body and knocked out windows, exposed its wheels to the sky. Heavy stones, scrap metal, broken furniture, torn up signs were scattered all over the streets. Barricades barred the way.

(My relative from Moscow told me that now this trolleybus is in Moscow's Museum of the October Revolution. This enormous mass of metal became an exhibit of history. Perhaps, the Museum provided a huge hall for this "tiny" evidence of the fight for power in the former Soviet Government.)

We could go no farther, and I didn't want to. For me it was too stressful and more than enough. I asked my children to continue their walk without me and turned into the first side street, trying to disconnect my senses from that horror. Calming down, I found a more or less peaceful place with a bench in the shade.

At 6 p.m. we returned to the Embassy and there got full permission to immigrate to America. In order to get this official permission, it usually took two to two and a half years. In our case only three and one-half months had passed since Washington accepted our applications in May. A miracle had happened.

Dear God, it was your will. My low bow to you, heavenly Father...

Did You Ever Have the Chance to Marry an American Multimillionaire?

Who can dare tell me that it was just a coincidence? I knew that God was with me. After this, I, a woman who grew up and lived all of my life in an atheistic society, started to believe in God.

❦

The Amazing Path

Before her departure Fiana had joked at the door about American applications; I miraculously found them at my home. Now I am a citizen of the United States of America. I am an American. The cherished dream came true. America showed us its generous hospitality. We got the many benefits this wonderful country offered to refugees and could enjoy our existence in this American paradise. But this paradise was only in our imagination before we landed in the United States.

The reality appeared much crueler. First came the understanding that there is no perfect society in the world. Second, it was tremendously difficult to change everything in our life: country, home, language, friends, habits, and customs. In order to survive we must remodel ourselves. A torrent of new events and a volcano of emotions, admiration and disillusion, trust and betrayal, support and ignorance, love and displeasure, appreciation of new wonderful friends and disappointment in old ones, suspense, frustration, perseverance—emigration means all of these, plus much more. This is my feeling about immigration.

CHAPTER 17

Della wrote this story in her college class. Herbert edited it. He read it with tears.

"You really went through hell. You have such a strong personality, you are such a powerful woman, Dellishka. I am proud of you and you must be proud of yourself. To make this by yourself, without any help? With a broken right shoulder and having an elderly aunt to take care of? You are a hero! You are outstanding, I have no words. Now you need to nourish yourself like a delicate orchid. And I will do it for you. I promise I will do my best to please you, my darling."

"Herbertchik, dear, it really was so hard, believe me, I am not powerful at all, I am a very weak woman. I just did what life pushed me to do. I did not have another choice. Honestly, you cannot imagine how exhausted I am. I feel like I never will get rid of this tiredness," Della sighed.

"My darling, it was all in the past. It is gone. Drop it! Forever! Forget it!"

"Do you know how I broke my shoulder? I wanted to buy nice gifts to bring to my relatives in America. We had a good store on the outskirts of the city, near the sea. Somebody told me that they had French perfume there. It took forty minutes on the tram to get to that store. So, I came, bought a few bottles of very nice French perfume for a lot of money, being proud of myself that I made it, and thinking that my American relatives would be very satisfied with my gifts.

"On my way out of the store there was a short pedestal on the floor. It was only a few inches high. I didn't notice it, and I stumbled and fell. Usually when we fall, we instinctively bend our two hands toward the floor to protect ourselves. But in my right hand was the bag with the bottles of expensive French perfume and to protect the bottles, I intuitively stretched my right hand forward. I saved the perfume, but broke my right shoulder. Emergency took me to the hospital.

Did You Ever Have the Chance to Marry an American Multimillionaire?

"We already had our tickets to America. In a couple of months or so we were to fly to New York, while a million things needed to be taken care of in the meantime. But instead I was in this damn hospital bed with awful pain. To my own surprise, I somehow felt relieved. I was so exhausted with the preparation for immigration that this time spent on a hospital bed became a blessing for me.

"After I was released from the hospital they sent me to physical therapy. The therapist worked with my shoulder so carefully, that now I don't feel like I ever broke it. My shoulder healed so well that, honestly, now I think it was God's will to arrange this shoulder's "event" for me. Those few weeks that I was not able to do anything but rest was just what I needed. Otherwise, I don't know how I would have been able to survive such intense exertion.

"And you know what happened to the expensive French perfume, Herbertchik? Something heartbreaking. When I presented this perfume to my relative in San Diego, a gift I was so proud of, she told me: 'Thank you, but I do not use this fragrance; I will give it to somebody else.' I was stunned. After all that I went through to get this for her."

"That's terrible, Dellishka," he said, giving her a soft kiss on her forehead. Then he smiled, trying to cheer her up, and said, "Forget it, darling. Tomorrow we are going to watch the opera *Eugene Onegin* by Tchaikovsky at the Civic Theater. It is gorgeous and you will adore it. Before that, we will have dinner in a nice restaurant near the ocean. I've already made reservations."

CHAPTER 18

"Eugene Onegin." Della studied this poem by Pushkin in high school. She knew it by heart. Bewitching, unforgettable sounds of Tchaikovsky. She watched this opera in Russia many times. Now it was an American version of *Eugene Onegin*.

In a Russian village, in a garden full of apple trees, young peasant women were cooking apple jam, singing beautiful Russian songs. But... Can you imagine Russian peasants being black? Black women on a farm of a remote Russian village in the middle of the 18th or 19th century? Impossible. They looked totally unreal for anybody who knew Russian culture. Yes, the women singers were black. This didn't match at all with a real Russian village.

The heroine of the opera, Tatyana, writes a letter to Eugene. She sings it. This is a main aria in the opera. Later investigations established that this Pushkin heroine Tatyana was about 13 years old, a romantic girl, who grew up in a village and was astonished by the appearance of a handsome, elegant young man from the Russian capital.

Being overwhelmed, she writes a love letter to him. The woman who played Tatyana's role in this opera performance may have been a famous singer and had a wonderful voice, but she was a heavy woman, a good 40-plus years old, and with dark skin. None of it fit what Della knew. Plus she wrote a letter with her left hand. At that time, you would not see left-handed people in Russia. If the child was born left handed, this child was specially trained to be right handed because the doctors thought that to be left handed was abnormal.

The American spectators never noticed these little details. To notice these distracting details, you had to look at the performance with Russian eyes. A few days later Herbert invited Della to another performance: *Fiddler on the Roof*. Tevye's wife was preparing the tea for the matchmaker by putting tea bags in the cups. No, at that time they did not have tea bags. They brewed the real tea in tea pots and from there put it into cups with

Did You Ever Have the Chance to Marry an American Multimillionaire?

saucers. Then they put hot tea from the cup into saucers to cool the tea. They sipped it loudly (very loudly!) from the saucers. This detail could have made the scene very funny and real.

Della said to Herbert that these small details were important and perhaps the director of the show did not know about them. She asked him to go with her behind the stage so she could inform the director. Embarrassed, Herbert told Della that they didn't have time, and led her away from the stage.

"Did you like the show otherwise, Dellishka?"

"Oh, yes! I loved it!" gushed Della, happily. "Simply loved it! Thank you, my Herbertchik."

Della was so grateful that Herbert appeared in her life. He was a good listener, smart and wise, gave her priceless advice, and tried to help as much as possible in any situation in her new life in this new country. She trusted him with all her worries. Della no longer needed to call Jewish Family Services to send a volunteer to take Rachel to a doctor's appointment. Herbert always offered a ride, and then patiently waited at the doctor's office to take her home. But Della did not feel comfortable when he, a busy man, spent so much time on account of Rachel.

"Dellishka, darling, it is my pleasure to spend this time with you and to make you feel comfortable. It is my pleasure to see you, to be near you," he always answered.

Do you wonder whatever happened to Jacob-Yasha? Where is he in this story? Nowhere. He stopped calling Della once he knew that Della was dating Herbert. Herbert, as Jacob's landlord, told Della that Jacob had stopped paying rent for his room.

"Maybe he doesn't pay you because he thinks that you are obligated to him for introducing me to you," Della mentioned.

"Yes, I know this. But still, it's not right," Herbert replied.

"Yes, I agree. If he doesn't understand, perhaps you better talk to him." A month later Jacob vacated Herbert's office, and Della's life, as well.

CHAPTER 19

It is interesting to look at our life as a performance. When the time is right, somebody new appears on our life's stage or previous actors return to play a different role in our existence. We simultaneously must be directors and actors in our own life-play. We should coordinate all collisions and participants of this play right now; our reaction has to be quick and spontaneous. There are no rehearsals in this performance. If we are unable to use previous experience or we don't have enough inner intuition, we make harmful mistakes.

By the wheel of fortune, Herbert came into Della's life in the very beginning of her immigration. He became the main hero in Della's new American life-play. Did she meet people here, in San Diego, whom she knew before, back in Odessa? Oh, yes, definitely, she did. Very dear people.

But as it said, nothing is truly learned until it is lived. Immigration can change people's behavior. Some of these loved one's reaction to Della's relationship with Herbert was strange. Perhaps it was jealousy. Della went through a lot of pain and betrayals with people she cared about. The closest friends betrayed her, and the strangers helped tremendously. If friends betray us, it is the same that they break our arms. We can forgive them, but we cannot embrace them again.

Not wanting to dwell on her disappointments, she just sent them her blessings and put them aside. It was not easy to do. Dear people take a big space in our heart; letting them go caused emotional trauma. Well, this was life's reality that not always has been painted in pink colors. Della concentrated her affection on Herbert and the many new people she was meeting that accepted her.

There were so many really important things Della had to take care as a newcomer to America. English! She did not permit herself to read any Russian words. Only English. She pushed herself to think in English. It was easy near Herbert. Her thoughts started to hover in her head with an English accent and English sound.

Many new friends and activities came into Della's life. She attended free classes at Mid-City College, having wonderful teachers and meeting students from all over the world. She immersed herself in her studies: conversation classes, English grammar, pronunciation, and computer courses.

So many things she needed to learn. Plus, with all of these new, extremely interesting and absolutely necessary obligations that Della was required to accept, to learn and to digest, there was old helpless Rachel waiting at home in desperate need for Della's constant assistance.

Della's days were so packed with duties, that by the time she went to bed at night, she was so exhausted that she couldn't move a finger. But when Herbert came, she knew she must be fresh and cheerful. This was a promise she made to herself.

Over time, all of these duties that she carried became torture for Della. She understood that she had to find an easier way to meet her obligations without being so tense, to learn to relax, to be more organized and not waste time and energy on unneeded things. This became a big priority for her. She realized that she must change something in herself, but how?

Her past bothered her terribly, but she didn't want to exhume any stinking memories. Who needs to live in a rotten past? She wanted to forget about it forever. But how could she make these changes, if her memories controlled her?

She tried to look at everything with a good sense of humor and a cheerful frame of mind, but it wasn't always possible.

Della talked to herself:

Listen, you are a volcano, a Vesuvius, where lava is boiling, ready to explode. You can blow up once and make a big disaster in America.

She taught herself:

You are in America! You are not in agony anymore. Now is the time to laugh at your unhappy past. Blow it off!

It helped somehow. Della squared her shoulders, deeply breathing in the fresh air of America. She knew that she must go through tremendous psychological changes through times of trial, to go from weakness to strength, from suffering to compassion, from lonely fear to the courage of faith. She was ready for it. She understood she must take this new huge step, but she couldn't imagine how hard it would be to do in everyday life.

CHAPTER 20

Della and Herbert just had lunch in the Marriott Hotel in Seaport Village. The Marriott usually offered a great Sunday Brunch and Herbert loved to take Della there.

It was a gorgeous day, and they went to the pool area, a wonderful place, decorated with fantastic plants, little waterfalls and caves. They were sitting in comfortable chairs, relaxing and enjoying the beautiful view.

"I know it was not easy in the USSR. You told me a little bit about your life there. Would you like to tell me more, Dellishka?" Herbert asked.

"Herbertchik, as I told you before, it won't be a pleasure for you if I continue to talk about my past. Why do you need to listen to all this crap?"

"You need to get this off your chest. It's better to talk about unpleasant things in a pleasant environment. You will feel better. So, go ahead, talk to me."

"Do you really need to know all the chaotic junk I went through?"

"I want to know everything about you."

"Well, maybe I need to talk it out. I really have too much on my mind." She closed her eyes in memory, then she began.

"I lived in a country with a terrible system, but we actually did not know how really terrible it was. We were isolated from the entire world, and did not have much information about life in Western countries. But when Gorbachev came to power, many things changed. There was a crash in the country, nobody expected it, and there was a crash in my personal life as well. Do you really want to hear all this?"

"Yes, Dellishka, I feel that you must talk about this. Do not keep it inside. You will feel better."

Della gratefully looked at Herbert.

"Okay, if you say so." Della took a deep breath, then she continued. "I went through many crashes, not one. The crash in the Soviet Union applied not only to me. In the end of the 1980s the new government became brave and decided to tell the truth about the deeds of the Communist Party. They named it 'Glasnost', that meant 'openness'. People had heart and learned so many terrible things that their hair stood up on their head. It was impossible to understand how the system could make everybody so duped and fooled during their entire lives.

"A flood of ugly stories poured from the radio, TV, newspapers and magazines. Normal human beings couldn't perceive the amount of cruelty that was going on in the country since the October Revolution of 1917. This saying says it best: 'They were so open minded that their brains fall out.' Everyone felt soiled by what had been going on. It was as if we were in a muddy puddle filled with a dirty, stinky, sticky mess that was impossible to wash off. These crazy muddles depressed everybody in the USSR.

"My family also fell apart. The divorce was tremendously difficult. This divorce was the greatest victory in my life. It didn't matter to me that in the eyes of all my relatives and closest friends I was viewed as a failure. My best friends and family abandoned me. Everybody. A huge emptiness grew around me, bigger and bigger. It brought years of emotional pain. So very painful. I was not able to deal with this pain. No one doctor could help me, no one pill. I do not want to talk about this."

Hebert hugged her and pulled her tightly to his chest.

"Cry! Cry it out! Cry loudly!" Herbert whispered in her ear.

"I would be glad to, but I cannot. I forgot how to cry." Then she stretched out her arm and waved it around the beautiful patio. "Here is such a beautiful day, Herbertchik. Let's enjoy it. When we go back to the past, we live it again, and we miss the present. No! I do not want to go there. Let's go home. Rachel is waiting for me. She is probably hungry."

"Can she take something from the refrigerator to eat?"

"She can, but it would be better if I give her a full meal." Herbert offered her his hand, and they left.

That night Della could not sleep. She was so sorry that she told Herbert all this stuff.

He is American, he doesn't need to know all the troubles I went through, Della chided herself.

Did You Ever Have the Chance to Marry an American Multimillionaire?

In the middle of the night she went into the bathroom; she looked at herself in the mirror.

I talked about this with him because he asked me and because I needed to talk it out. He was right. Now it is his will and his choice to react to this kindly or not.

She looked deeply into her own eyes, talking with her inner-self. *Actually, you did not tell him anything. You told him nothing! If you start to talk loudly about what you went through, you will make yourself sick. No way! No! No! Forget about your past! Do not relive it again! It is over! Period!*

◈

The next day Herbert took Della to Balboa Park, a beautiful place in San Diego. After lunch they went to the Rose Garden, chose a cozy place, enjoying the greenery, blue sky, and gorgeous roses.

"Herbertchik, yesterday I told you some unpleasant things in my life. Yes, I went through big hardships. By the way, I recently read somewhere that hardships often prepare an ordinary person for an extraordinary destiny. Who knows, maybe it is true. Actually, your appearance in my life is definitely extraordinary."

Herbert hugged her. "I will do everything to make you happy. You keep a lot inside of you. Too much. It is past, it is gone, and you need to find a way to get rid of this. It is serious. Our conversation yesterday awoke in me old memories. I could not sleep. Now let me tell you my story."

Della turned towards him and put her hand on his.

"I grew up in Pennsylvania, in an Orthodox Jewish family. My father was very religious. I graduated from the university there. I wanted to be a radio announcer and made it. My father was not happy with me. I was not so good in Orthodox Jewish Torah teachings. But he had another two sons, my brothers, and one of my nephews became a rabbi. So, my father was somehow satisfied. I wanted to live my own life and decided to move to California. I was young and not experienced. Being a radio announcer gave me satisfaction for a few years, but I understood that I would never make money with this and searched for something different.

"I moved to San Diego, and met a woman here. She was 15 years older than me, and had been married two times. She had three children: a 17-year-old boy, Al, from the first marriage; and two little kids from the last marriage: a 6-year-old girl, Dina, and a 2- year-old boy, Clint. I became very attached to this woman and her kids. She was smart, beautiful, full of energy, a great businesswoman, and had a jewelry store.

"She became my everything. She was my lover. I was young and not very experienced, she taught me love. She was my teacher. She taught me so many useful things about life. And maybe she was sometimes even a mama to me. She opened a door for me to another world. We were deeply in love. I proposed to her, and she accepted. We did not tell anybody about our decision, we just became married. I was 25, she was 40.

"When her relatives found this out, they became furious. They continuously called her to scold her:

'What did you do? You married a boy. He is just a few years older than your oldest son. He married you because of your money. He will rob you and you will be left with nothing. You have three children, you did not think about them!' And so on and so on... They poured much blame on our heads.

"My wife became pregnant. With this news they became even angrier and the division in her family grew more.

"'Why do you need another child? You already have three. Don't you understand that you are much older than him? This fellow is smart. With your help he will establish himself in San Diego and then will wave you 'goodbye' with your four kids. You are just a springboard for him to make a jump into San Diego society. And when it happens, you'll be left behind. You are so stupid!'

"My wife, a strong woman, cried at night. 'Why is it their business, why are they so angry and unkind? I love them so much, they are my dearest people. I do not want to be such a disappointment to them.'

"My wife was five months pregnant. With all these worries she lost the baby. It was a little boy. I would now have a 43-year-old son. After this, she was not able to have any children."

Did You Ever Have the Chance to Marry an American Multimillionaire?

Herbert paused and wiped his eyes. Della patted his hand. Then he sighed and continued.

"We broke with her family forever. She was strong. I lived with my wife for 43 years. For all these years we did not allow anybody from her family to enter our house. It was her firm decision, very, very painful for her and for me too. So, I know, Dellishka, how it feels when all your dearest people abandon and betray you. You are not alone."

"You know, Herbertchik, people are people, we cannot change them. There is a great prayer:

'God, give me the ability to accept people I cannot change.
Help me to change the person I can change.
Give me the wisdom to understand
that this person is only myself.'

"Thank you, my darling Dellishka. Let us go home."

CHAPTER 21

Christmas was around the corner. Herbert was an active Shriner for many years and invited Della to their special Christmas party. He came dressed in a tuxedo and Della was in a gorgeous dress and shoes that Herbert bought for her a few days earlier.

When Della and Herbert entered the hall with sparkling lights, she gasped. Never before had she seen anything as solemn and ceremonial. A special red-golden hat embellished Herbert's head. They were ushered to their table and took their seats. On the table were elegantly written cards which read: Mr. Herbert Samson and Lady Della Samson.

Della took a few deep breaths and told herself:

"Okay, Lady Della Samson, if you are here in this role, please behave and play it as if you were born a queen! No less! You look gorgeous, young, magnificent, with beautiful red curls crowning your head.

Today the beautician did a great job with your hair. Now these red curls are just to the point. You are definitely more beautiful than other women at this table and at this party."

Della squared her shoulders, lifted her head, and with a charming smile started to chat with people at the table. She talked with an accent. They asked where she was from and what her profession was. Herbert answered proudly:

"My wonderful lady is an engineer-designer and worked many years in the movie industry."

Everybody looked at Della with admiration. They started to ask her in what movies she participated.

"No, I did not participate in any movie. I am not an actress; I am an engineer-designer. I worked in a big office that designed equipment to make movies. We designed machines to make cartoons, to make perforations in the film, to rotate the film, special tables to check the films, and

Did You Ever Have the Chance to Marry an American Multimillionaire?

many other devices and appliances. It was very precise and complicated equipment. We designed everything except cameras.

Cameras were sent to us from other factories. I had a very interesting job. Our office was respectful and big, but then it started to fall apart like everything else in the Soviet Union. Sad."

The dinner was over. A piano player opened the piano and started to play dancing music. Herbert enjoyed music. They danced. Almost each dance somebody asked Herbert's permission to invite his lady for a waltz or a tango.

Della watched Herbert. His eyes, his face, each movement expressed his delight.

"Dellishka, you are wonderful. How can you amaze and attract everybody?"

Dancing with her, holding her close, he whispered compliments in her ear. She whispered in his ears back:

"Because of you, my darling. Only because of you. You lifted me up. I am just helping you to show all your friends and guests here what an outstanding lady you have in your arms right now."

"My arms will keep you tightly forever, Dellishka. The more I know you, the more I realize how great you are as a person and as a woman. You are a lady of a very high level. You belong here. And do not forget that this is one of the highest strata of American society. Yes, you belong here, no doubt."

She laughed:

"Certainly. Where else would Lady Della Samson belong?"

Herbert kissed her passionately right in the middle of the dance.

"You are such a hot, sexy man. Look, all the other men are jealous of you."

"Who cares? Let them all be jealous."

He whispered this to Della, then continued passionately kissing her.

"Women are jealous too. Don't let them be jealous. Please, invite somebody to dance."

"What for? No way! I want you, only you, and forever you. You are the most gorgeous lady I have ever met. And, my queen, I made us reservations for New Year's Eve in the Crown Room at the Hotel Del Coronado. There you will be part of high society, my darling! It will be your peak!"

"No, Herbertchik, it will be my trampoline, it will be our trampoline, our ski-jump!"

"You are really something, Dellishka! You are outstanding!"

Herbert talked to her, smiling into her eyes. He held her so tightly that she felt herself as an inalienable part of him.

CHAPTER 22

DELLA'S BIRTHDAY WAS just the day after Christmas. She laughed:

"I let Jesus Christ come first to the world, then he opened the gate for me and I arrived after him on Dec. 26, helping Jesus make this world more beautiful."

They often came for dinner to the Rusty Pelican restaurant. Della admired the colorful decorations and enjoyed eating there a lot. Herbert said:

"Your birthday is coming. Let's throw a party in this place. Invite your relatives; it might dissolve the growing tension between you."

"Good idea, Herbertchik. Back in Odessa we celebrated all our birthday parties together until they departed to America. We always had very warm gatherings."

Della called her uncle and his two children, her cousins.

"Do you still remember when my birthday is?"

"Of course, we do."

Della's first birthday lunch-party in America. Back in Odessa she could not afford to invite her guests to a restaurant. A restaurant like the Rusty Pelican would be an unreachable dream in Odessa. Usually Della made her birthday parties at home, where she prepared a lot of food all by herself. When guests came, she was deadly tired, but the atmosphere at the table was always cheerful; everybody laughed, enjoying each other. The last celebration was in Odessa, 15 years ago. Quick as a blink, fifteen years of their lives sped by. Della and her relatives were different people now. How would this reunion go here in America? She did not know.

The day of the party, Herbert arrived at the restaurant with Della and Rachel. Della freshened herself up in the little mirror on the window visor, and when she was satisfied, she stepped out and walked towards the restaurant. Herbert wheeled Rachel in, and seated her at the table next to her brother, just like many years ago in Odessa. Everyone greeted each other with hugs, and made conversation as they sat at the table waiting for the food to arrive. The table was set gorgeously. The candles sparkled on the table. And the food was tasty and beautifully served. But the mood... what happened? They couldn't create the same joyful mood as it had been in Odessa. Between the laughter and the jokes, there were awkward silences. Herbert, being a smart man and as host of the party (certainly, he paid for everybody), tried his best to ease the atmosphere. He hugged Della, repeating: "My Birthday Girl. My Queen. Everyone, welcome. Enjoy yourselves, please."

Della looked around the table at all these people most dear to her, and yet she did not feel like a queen at all. She talked and laughed, but each particle of her skin felt that her relatives were not the same people she had known in Odessa. Everything was different. There was distance between them now, a growing gap, and she did not have a clue how to recapture the years of intimacy that used to be.

Later that night, as Della was reflecting about the evening, she told herself: *Do not be surprised. It is not only their fault. You are also definitely different and not the same as you had been in Odessa. This is life. Immigration changes people and changes relationships. If something doesn't go your way, there is a reason. Trust to your fate. Trust God. Forgive, and let it go.*

Days rushed by. The year 1992, little by little, dissolved into eternity. Herbert decided to make Della's first New Year's in America the most delightful and memorable experience ever. He wanted her to remember it for the rest of her life.

"We will celebrate the New Year's party at the Hotel Del Coronado. The next day, on January 1st, a gorgeous Rose Parade will be in Pasadena. They do it each year. Would you like to go?" Herbert asked Della. She did not know what it was, so she was hesitant to answer.

Did You Ever Have the Chance to Marry an American Multimillionaire?

"It is beautiful, Dellishka. They make fantastic moving floats designed with thousands of roses and other flowers." Della's eyes lit up. "The only problem is that we need to get there very early. We need to leave here around 5am to get to Pasadena, two hours away, and have a good space to watch the parade. A tremendous crowd comes to see it every year."

"We can get up early," Della assured him.

"If we are going to celebrate the New Year's Eve party, it will be tough. Once we get situated in Pasadena, we'd have to stand in the streets for a few hours until the parade starts. And it can be very cold in the morning. We can take folding chairs, but if we are sitting we won't see anything. And to carry the chairs from the car will not be easy, because who knows where we will find parking? People will stand in front of us and we won't be able to see much. Too big a crowd."

"So what do you suggest?" asked Della.

"In this case, it's better to watch it on TV."

Della laughed. "Herbertchik, thanks to you, I have a gorgeous TV now. Plus, I don't want to leave Rachel alone on the first day of the New Year."

On New Year's Eve, at 6:30pm, they arrived at the Hotel Del Coronado, the most prestigious and expensive place in San Diego.

"I can't wait to see how they've decorated the ballroom for New Year's. I've had such fun looking forward to this night," Della said, her eyes sparkling. Then she kissed Herbert on the cheek and hooked her arm into his.

For the second time this year, they entered the Crown Room. Della expected the gorgeous dining hall to glitter with a lot of lights and be gaily decorated. But, no, to her surprise there was not much light. The decoration was made up mostly of black balloons, very subdued. A black hat for a man and a crown with white feathers for the lady, two little horns, and two black and white rattles were laid out on their table.

Their dining table was tiny; they hardly could place their dishes on it. The table itself donned a snow-white tablecloth and black linen napkins to match the balloons. *For what reason had the decorators decided to use the color black?* She knew that people paid big money to be here to celebrate New Year's Eve, one of the happiest times of the year. The color black just didn't fit the gay spirit. *Who can really understand these Americans?* Della thought.

As a newcomer, Della watched everybody and everything, noticed each little detail in such an expensive place. The reason for such small tables? Every seat cost a fortune, so, she figured, the more tables, the more people could be seated, and the more money for the restaurant.

Della looked at the people. The average age was about fifty-plus. Probably, only at this age, could people afford such a lavish New Year's Eve party. All the women were well dressed, many with sparkling diamonds and magnificent furs. Della never saw so many diamonds and jewels on women in her whole life. Della was wearing a gorgeous black evening dress. Even if she didn't have diamonds and furs, she was confident she matched this company very well. And who cared? Della understood a long time ago that people usually cared only about how they looked, not how anybody else looked.

Della's thoughts danced their own dance in her head. She asked herself: *Where am I? How did I appear here? Who are these rich people? And here I am among them. Amazing...* Della looked at Herbert. *Is he a millionaire too?*

"Herbertchik, are all these people millionaires?"

"Why do you ask me this question?"

"I don't know. I am just curious. How about you? Are you a millionaire?"

"Stop thinking silly thoughts, darling. Let us see what appetizers they brought us to eat."

"Why did you change the subject? Just tell me 'Yes' or 'No'."

"Better we order the dinner! I am hungry."

He looked in the menu with fancy dishes with intricate names. Della was not able to understand the description of the food.

"I need a dictionary to understand the names of the dishes. I will study this menu tomorrow with the dictionary," Della laughed, as she put the menu in her purse as a souvenir.

"Not to worry," Herbert said, "I will order for both of us."

Did You Ever Have the Chance to Marry an American Multimillionaire?

The waiter brought the dinner on huge, beautiful plates with a tiny amount of fancy food on them. He set these gigantic plates on their little table. The food was prepared in interesting ways and was beautifully presented. Della took a bite. She was not sure what she was eating, but it was very tasty. Even so, she was too tense to eat.

"Why am I so nervous? Relax!" Della talked to herself, trying to stop this unwanted tension. Again, she recognized that even good changes could be stressful.

"This evening is supposed to be the best in my life. It is my triumph! Many Americans live their entire lives in San Diego, but never dare even to think about spending New Year's Eve in the Crown Room of the Hotel Del Coronado! Life sent me this gift: I am here! Relax immediately! Enjoy this moment! It has been given to me for all my sufferings!" She took a deep breath and blew out.

Della was not immediately able to relax physically, nor mentally, but still, she tried to shift her mood. Her connection with Herbert was so soulful, so precious, and this evening was meant to be one of those times when you look back and can legitimately say:

"Wow! That was one of the best days of my life!"

She felt Herbert's support and she was brave, talking with people in spite of her poor English. But inside... oh, she was a boiling volcano inside, even though she engaged all her inner power to look very calm.

Della clung to Herbert, grasping his hands.

"Hold me tight, Herbertchik!" she whispered to him. He understood how she felt, squeezed her in his arms, ardently kissed her eyes full with tears, and really did not care at all about the crowd of people around them.

"What did you do? You ruined all the makeup on my face," she smiled at him.

"Good! You look gorgeous anyway! You better eat, the food will be cold."

"I cannot, darling! I cannot swallow even a bite. I am sorry. Everything is new for me here. I am too overwhelmed."

"It is okay, my love. I sometimes forget you've only been here for five months. Look around. It will calm you down."

"Thanks for understanding. I will eat later, do not worry."

During the dinner the ballroom became alive with music. Vic Damone was the guest singer, and the Bill Green Orchestra performed their best. The guests ate, laughed, waltzed around the dance floor, and hugged each other—even people they had never met before.

Herbert cordially invited Della for their first waltz. They danced and danced and danced. Della hugged Herbert and still could not believe that she was here, in the arms of a great American man, in this wealthy restaurant, surrounded with music and happy people. She danced and laughed, laughed and danced... with tears.

"Am I in America, Herbert? I do not believe it..."

"You are, my darling. Do not cry!" Herbert kissed her eyes. "Yes, you are in America. And I am a real American, near you. And will be always! I will give you all the best I can. I will lift you up as high as possible. I will create my own shining throne for you."

They came back to the table. It was clean. The waiter had taken their plates away and prepared a bottle with Champagne and two sparkling glasses.

"You did not eat your dinner! I told you to eat. Now you are hungry," Herbert chided Della.

"I am fine. I will survive. Do not worry..." Della tried to cope with her emotions.

Finally midnight arrived! All the guests blew their little horns and shook their rattles, and yelled and screamed to welcome the New Year, 1993. This custom was new for Della, but she played with these toys with the enthusiasm of a little child.

A huge bundle of black balloons was released from the ceiling. Black balloons floated everywhere; they looked so festive. Herbert got up, came to Della, and raised her from the chair so they could sip their Champagne from one glass, lip to lip.

Did You Ever Have the Chance to Marry an American Multimillionaire?

After they drank the glass of Champagne, Della asked, "Will we eat soon, Herbertchik?" she asked.

"Eat? We had a dinner. To eat after midnight is not healthy."

"That dinner was in 1992, last year. Now it is 1993. In Russia we have the best food all New Year's night."

"You did not eat your dinner and now you are hungry as a wolf." Herbert waved the waiter over.

"My lady is hungry. Can you please bring her something to eat?"

The waiter ran to the kitchen and came back empty handed.

"I'm sorry, everything in the kitchen is locked and everybody left."

Della laughed: on her first New Year's Eve in America, in the richest country in the world, in the most prestigious and expensive restaurant, she couldn't get a little bite of food.

"You see, Herbertchik, now the whole year I will be hungry. You made me starve in America," Della teased him.

The romantic music beckoned them, and they returned to the middle of the hall and danced, and whirled, and danced some more.

"Keep me tight, Herbertchik!" Della repeated.

"I will, my darling! Always!"

They noticed that they were dancing in an almost empty hall.

It was 12:30 a.m. People had already started to leave. The celebration was over. One half hour later the ballroom was empty.

They were sitting at their table. The musicians still played, but they did not want to dance. Della talked animatedly, comparing her American New Year's experience with the Russian customs of celebrating New Year's Eve.

"In Russia it is completely different. People come together on December 31 about 10:30 p.m., enjoying each other. About 11:30 they raise their glasses to say 'Goodbye' to the old year, talking about the good and not so good things that had happened in the departing year. The table is full of viands that were prepared special. Then at 12 midnight we drink our Champagne—or wine, or brandy, or vodka—welcoming the New Year, and then we eat, and drink, and dance all night. That way we feel that the coming year will be filled with delicious food, with good wine, and with good feelings."

Herbert listened intently. Della saw he was sincerely interested, so she continued.

"Young people stay longer, the elderly become tired and leave sooner, but it is usually uncommon in Russia to leave a special New Year's Eve party right after the New Year arrives."

With that, Herbert filled their Champagne glasses for the last time. They clinked their glasses together, and smiled at each other as they sipped the last of the sparkling drink.

"Let's go home and I will show you how to celebrate a New Year," Della said.

On their drive home Della sang. She did not know English songs; she sang in Russian. Herbert tried to follow the Russian words. It sounded so funny. Della laughed and sang, and again laughed.

Herbert looked at her with so much love and admiration.

"Do not look at me! You are driving, look at the road, not at me. Please!"

"What the heck is the road? You are my road!" Herbert responded.

Once they settled in at home, Della opened the refrigerator, spread all her delicious goodies on the table, and then they really started to celebrate the New 1993 Year.

Later, in bed, Herbert, not a young man, surprised Della with his unbelievably strong man's abilities and potency. This night was the highest point of their happiness, the mountain they climbed together, ready to embrace the entire Universe.

In the morning, they watched the Rose Parade. They were together, silently enjoying each other. They did not want to talk, just to feel each other's closeness and warmth. Rachel was sitting nearby in her armchair, amazed by the colors and beauty of the Rose Parade.

Herbert took Della for a walk to Harbor Island and for dinner at Tom Ham's Light House. On January 2, the second day of the New Year, they danced in Le Pavilion at the Town & Country Hotel. Indeed, Herbert

Did You Ever Have the Chance to Marry an American Multimillionaire?

knew very well the most beautiful places in San Diego to enjoy life and entertain Della.

And to help her always remember this special time, Della took the Crown Room's New Year's Eve Menu out of her purse, kissed it, and then slipped it inside of an album full of mementos and priceless photographs.

—•—

Unbelievable things happen in life. Could Della have imagined at that time, on the Eve of the year 1993, that 22 years later, in the year 2015, a writer would write a book about her adventures in America? Certainly, not. And do you know what? Yes, unpredictable things happen. Twenty-two years later she found the menu of that New Year's dinner and wanted it included in this book. She had a remarkable story to tell.

"In May of 2011, I had a disaster happen to my apartment. The neighbor above had a huge fire, and the water the firefighters used to put out the fire penetrated through the walls and into my place and all my belongings were damaged by water and had to be thrown away. A total loss! In this soggy mess, only some papers were saved. Amazingly, this menu was found between old papers." She looked at the menu in her hand. "Is this an historical document? Who knows? Maybe."

Then she mused, "How many absolutely unneeded things do we keep in our closets for years, cluttering our home, and as a result, cluttering our life?" She shrugged her shoulders. "But, as you can see, cluttering sometimes has its own good reasons."

Then she laughed and laughed, appreciating all the delights that life's twists and turns presents us.

Dora Klinova

CHAPTER 23

THE HOLIDAY RUSH was over. Della understood that somehow the wheel of fortune had put her on the top of San Diego's society. In order to function on a certain level in her daily life, she realized she needed to make inner transitions, in addition to all the studying and learning she was doing to live in this new country. To feel equal to the people Herbert introduced to her, including his children and their families, she needed to convince herself that, yes, this was definitely the place where she was supposed to be at this time of her life.

It was not easy. Della repeated to herself again and again: "I deserve to be here. God put me here for a reason. It is my birth right to be with these people."

It was an awfully hard 24/7 inner job. While this inner work began to give her power, it was also draining and exhausting her. Too many things demanded her attention. She did not let herself pamper her tiredness. She felt better being busy. She just tried hard to do her best.

Since she lived in a new country, she knew she needed to behave differently, to act differently, and, most important of all, to *THINK* differently. Oh, it was so challenging, so difficult.

Della did not know it at the time that she had intuitively started to learn the spiritual art of inner improvement and transformation, a path that would serve her well for the rest of her life.

Rachel… Her aunt was so happy that Herbert appeared in Della's life. It also changed her life for the better, as well.

Della was a wonderful cook, and she liked to do it, so she often made dinners at home. The three of them sat around the table and ate tasty food together most nights, talking and laughing. Herbert always tried to entertain Rachel and spoke to her in Yiddish. His Yiddish was poor; he mixed it with English, which didn't help. Rachel did not hear well and did not understand what he was talking about, but they somehow made their conversations about who-knows-what. This always caused Della to choke from laughter. They both did not understand why Della laughed, but her laughter was contagious and soon they would join her with their own loud laughter.

When Herbert was there, it was always a cheerful atmosphere in their apartment.

Della looked at Rachel, at her happy face. In her wildest dreams, this old woman couldn't predict that she would be sitting at the table with an American conversing with him. Handicapped Rachel broke her hip in Odessa in 1982. Back in Odessa she had two surgeries but the hip was never healed. Rachel became unable to take care of herself and live alone. She had no children; Della was the only one who could help her. At that time in Odessa there were no facilities for sick, elderly people. Their relatives kept them at home and were supposed to take care of them. Often it was a huge burden for the family, but this was how it was.

When Rachel broke her hip, Della herself was recovering from a very serious surgery, but without any hesitation she took Rachel to her home and put her in one of the bedrooms of her two-bedroom apartment.

Della loved Rachel. With Rachel she could discuss many pleasant and unpleasant things. Rachel was a good listener. Della tried to comfort her as much as possible, and Rachel felt very nourished near Della. In Odessa it was a big challenge for Della to take care of Rachel: working a full time job as an engineer-designer, standing in lines in every store, and commuting on overcrowded buses. Working as an engineer, she was not able to afford a car. A car was an unattainable dream.

Did You Ever Have the Chance to Marry an American Multimillionaire?

To take Rachel out from the Soviet Union became a drama. It seemed that the Soviet Union could not survive without Rachel and her crutches. In order to begin the process of immigration for Rachel, Soviet authorities demanded her Birth Certificate; Rachel's passport was not enough for them. Where could Della get a Birth Certificate for an 82-year-old woman who was born before the revolution and before the Second World War somewhere in a remote Yiddish *shtatle*, *a village*, that probably didn't exist on the map anymore? Impossible! But the Soviet immigration authorities were firm. They required a Birth Certificate. Period. Somebody advised Della to write to the synagogue of the county where that *shtatle* was listed in the past. The synagogue was supposed to have archives.

Della did not believe that this synagogue still existed, and if yes, it hardly had any archives because that place was occupied by Nazis during World War Two. Nazis usually destroyed synagogues. Della could not even remember how she found the address of that synagogue, but she did, and, without any hope, she wrote a letter to them.

It took a year and a half of writing letters back and forth until, amazingly, they found Rachel in their archives and Rachel's Birth Certificate was sent to Della's address. Unbelievable! God had helped her and this impossible miracle happened. Della spent so much energy and many months to get this certificate that it became a treasure. A crazy treasure of Soviet reality. Below you can see this Birth Certificate that Della dug out from a remote Yiddish village in Ukraine. Rachel was born in 1911, but this Birth Certificate was issued in 1991. Yes, it is a crazy treasure.

Finally, Soviet authorities were satisfied with this certificate, but not America. America simply did not welcome Rachel because they only gave permission to direct relatives as a plan of reuniting family. Rachel was just an aunt to Della. To break this wall, Della dared to call the Washington Immigration Center explaining that handicapped Rachel lived with her and could not be left alone in the Soviet Union. Miraculously, Washington gave Della special permission to bring Rachel to the United States! Again, only with God's help!

Rachel's mind was good, but her vision and hearing became weak. She was getting terribly bored. So, Della ordered a new telephone with large numbers and increased volume. Now Rachel could talk with her relatives any time she wanted. It became her main amusement.

Della understood that Rachel discussed on the telephone back and forth each of Herbert's visits and Della's every movement in life. What else she could talk about? The fantasy of half-blind and half-deaf Aunt Rachel

Did You Ever Have the Chance to Marry an American Multimillionaire?

was in its fullest expression. She created cock-and-bull stories about Della's admirer and shared them with the relatives. Information about Della's personal life that was given to relatives began spreading through the large Russian community in San Diego. One time, some Russian people whom Della barely knew started to ask her questions about the rich American man she was dating. Della was shocked with their unpardonable curiosity about her personal life. She knew that the main source of the gossip was Rachel. She talked to Rachel, forbidding her to say anything about Herbert. It did not help. Della was not able to stop Rachel's phone calls.

Yes, Rachel felt very comfortable near Della, but how did Della feel about Rachel? Understandably, taking care of her aunt was a huge burden on her shoulders that ended up lasting for many years. Growing older, Rachel was becoming so difficult and uncooperative, that it made things even harder for Della.

Plus poor Rachel became mixed up in America. Before she received her pension in rubles, now the American government assisted her in dollars. Wow! She received dollars, the most valuable currency in the world! If her small amount of dollars would be transferred into rubles she could be a millionaire in Odessa. Being bored at home, Rachel counted her money. It became her best entertainment when she was not gossiping on the phone.

Because all her life she was used to rubles, Rachel counted her SSI Welfare in rubles. The amount in rubles made her feel much better and she became more demanding. Della watched how her kind aunt was being changed. An old, sick, helpless woman whom Della loved dearly was making Della's life extremely limited. What could she do about it?

Could Della give her away to a caring facility here, in San Diego? Yes, she could. But Rachel would not be able to live there because she did not know any English. Absence of communication would kill her. No, Della couldn't do that to Rachel.

CHAPTER 24

By arriving to America, Della stepped away from the Soviet Union's dirty mess. Even so, her spirit was drained and she arrived feeling devastated. She hoped that by living in a new country, she could neatly pack away the painful memories of the past, and never have to visit them again. But how could she accomplish this in reality?

Her emotional pain refused to be buried. It manifested in profound bitterness. Especially at night. This anguish was much, much more than Della could bear. To get rid of this, Della decided to meditate. But the rush of thoughts in her head was more powerful than her persistent attempt to concentrate and focus.

How could she quiet this endless torrent of upsetting thoughts? Doctors could not help. The pills they prescribed did not work. The thoughts possessed her anyway.

Perhaps she could write out her anguish in a diary. She did. She also talked her troublesome thoughts into a little recording machine. She did everything that she could think of to get beyond her overwhelmed mind.

"Listen, big thinker, most of the time your thinking is useless, you are wasting energy. If you create this current of thoughts, you must be able to stop this current."

She tried desperately, but could not. She welcomed her good sense of humor.

It helped somehow.

Della studied English and didn't permit herself to read anything in Russian, being afraid to waste any minute of her time from mastering English. Her brains were overloaded with all this new information.

Did You Ever Have the Chance to Marry an American Multimillionaire?

In addition to her studies and desperately learning how to keep herself in a healthier state of mind, taking care of Rachel became a very hard task for Della.

In this situation Herbert was a gift from God for her. To give Herbert his due, he was ever willing to help. One night Rachel became sick and at 2 o'clock in the morning Della had to call Emergency. Della had to go with her to the hospital and she was scared. Rachel didn't know a word of English and Della's English was not good enough that she could understand all that the doctors were telling her. She was desperate for help. She dared to call Herbert, not her relatives. He arrived immediately, and stayed with them at the hospital all night. This generosity of Herbert's soul was invaluable for Della.

"My low bow to you, Herbertchik, for your kindness and emotional support. I will never forget it."

By now Herbert felt like he was a part of Della's family. He wanted to stay with her almost every night. Rachel was very happy because she had a companion in the evenings and didn't complain when he started to almost live in their apartment. Herbert received Rachel's "approval."

Della was happy. Her nights with Herbert were delightful. She had been a long time without a man, and became very attached to Herbert. She wanted him. And Herbert often told her that he never ever felt so passionate, even in his younger years. He couldn't understand what was happening to him.

"At my age? I can do it at my age? Unbelievable!" He repeated it again and again. He wanted to make love more and more, but was afraid. He became mixed up.

"It is not healthy at my age. I need to do it once a week or even more rarely."

"Who said this to you?"

"It is according to my age. I just know this."

"Are you happy when you make love?"

"Of course. What are you talking about?"

"I am happy too. You make me young. You make yourself young. You have your own choice: to follow the schedule of making love you created for yourself or to enjoy my every hug, my every kiss, my every touch. Every muscle of our bodies, every organ, must be in motion to be alive. Do you want to make a lifeless man of yourself? You can. Easily. I want us to be and to feel young. In any case, I will leave this Earth when my time comes and I want to wave goodbye to this life with a happy sparkle in my eyes."

"You are young anyway. And soo sexy!"

Della laughed. "Don't you like it?"

"Yes, certainly I do! But it can affect my health!" he stubbornly repeated this again and again.

"So, go to the doctor," Della said.

And he did. He asked his physician, "How can a woman be so sexual at this age?"

His doctor, a man approximately Della's age, who had just divorced his wife, immediately responded, "You are scared, I am not. Introduce me to her. I want to see her. I want her. Where is she?" the doctor laughed.

Herbert roared, telling Della about this conversation. She laughed too:

"Herbertchik, please introduce me to your doctor. When you are tired of me, and think it is not healthy, I will call him."

"My God, what should I do? You are a vortex. You will kill me."

Della joked, "Do you know what is the most respectful and honorable death for a man?"

"What?"

"Inside of the woman. When you are inside of me, you are in Heaven, aren't you? When your time comes, you will not need to ask God to take you to Heaven, you already will be there!"

Herbert laughed, but Della's voice became serious.

"On a high spiritual level sex is an exchange of male and female energy. It keeps hormones working and alive. In the evening I am usually deadly tired and want only to sleep. But I push myself hard and push you to give us this pleasure because I know how it is important to activate our hormones. Hormones make our mind and body feel young."

Did You Ever Have the Chance to Marry an American Multimillionaire?

Herbert was impressed with her reasoning. She made his heart sing. And yet he still struggled. He couldn't believe that he felt like such a young man; it just didn't seem right. And the intensity of his emotions when he was with Della overwhelmed him and confused him.

He decided he still needed outside advice. So once again he sought out the rabbi of his synagogue, and he told Della about their conversation.

"I told the rabbi, 'I feel such deep love at this age, and I'm still having a hard time accepting it.' And he said to me, 'The fact is you feel it. This is the answer.' He told me I was very lucky and to count my blessings."

Della was surprised. "Why did you need to speak to the rabbi again? Your soul is your best adviser, better than any rabbi. Why do you need the rabbi's approval for your happiness?"

But Herbert was glad that he had talked to the rabbi. In Herbert's mind, their conversations were sacred. It was as if he received a divine blessing.

Della whispered in his ears quietly:

"Herbertchik, darling, do not think about your age! Look at yourself! You are a young, handsome fellow. All of San Diego is jealous of me because you are near. You are a nice man, a goodhearted person. It is almost impossible to meet somebody nice. It happened for us, let us enjoy it and feel that we are in Seventh Heaven. We are together because it was meant to be. God sent us to each other for a reason."

She paused and looked at him so lovingly, and then she said,

"For both of us it is not an easy time now. Your wife died and without her you felt like a ship lost at the sea. I am in a new country, and perhaps without you I would feel lost, too. Your rabbi is right. It is really a blessing that we met each other at this period of our lives. We must both be grateful. Love is a glorious thing, we must praise our every moment together. Love makes people younger and healthier. It is extremely valuable at our age. I am also not eighteen anymore. I am grateful and give a thousand thanks to God for everything. I do it in my every prayer."

CHAPTER 25

THE YEAR 1993 gathered its speed. Days rushed by. Herbert was busy in his office and now he more often communicated with his children. He frequently invited them for dinner, trying to keep the family together. Sometimes Della prepared dinner at home; sometimes they all went out together to a nice restaurant. Della loved being with his family; they were really nice people.

Della's days were packed. She attended Mid-City College to study English, she had lots of homework to do, she spent as much time with Herbert as she could, but the bulk of her time was spent caretaking Rachel and trying to meet her needs. Before she rushed off to college in the morning, Della got up early to prepare everything for Rachel to be sure she was set for the day.

Rachel needed medical supplies, such as a special seat for the toilet, equipment for bathing, and many other things that the doctor prescribed. It was up to Della to order them, and she didn't know how to do it. Her poor English was a big obstacle. She called many times to one place, but they didn't understand her. It felt like the phone was her enemy; it would get so hot in her hand that, in frustration, she'd fling it angrily across the room, then pick it up, and again continue to try to make endless arrangements.

Sometimes she asked Herbert to make the calls for her, but she didn't want to bother him too much and tried to do everything by herself. Besides, he was not at all familiar with the process of meeting a refugee's needs and what the system required.

When Della and Rachel came to the United States as Jewish refugees, Jewish organizations sponsored them during their first four months. Now it was up to Della to establish Rachel and herself with everything this blessed America offered them.

As refugees, they were entitled to government support in the form of a small pension. This helped pay for the rental apartment and all the bills

Did You Ever Have the Chance to Marry an American Multimillionaire?

Della had to pay. Also, they were given medical insurance. Rachel, as an old person, was entitled to Medicare. All these benefits did not come automatically. To acquire them, Della had to fill out numerous applications, make appointments, and wait in lines. But she did not even know where to take these applications and where to go, and what she could do, what she couldn't. She had to learn the rules, and Jewish Family Services was a big help. Della again and again called there, went there, and talked to the social workers.

Herbert could see all the effort Della was making so she could receive services. However, he never told Della that his support would be more than enough and she could forget about government benefits. No, just the opposite. He encouraged and pushed her to make everything possible to get all the benefits. He drove her to many organizations in the early morning and stood in line with her among poor people. Moreover, if he took her to any government appointment, he always came in his old car and wore very casual clothes. These little signs made Della firmly resolve that she must be independent financially and not to rely on Herbert.

Della continuously thought about her situation with her darling American man. Being realistic, she understood that he was willing to help her now, but what would happen tomorrow, nobody could predict. Her relationship with Herbert was not supported with any official papers and could burst like a soap bubble at any time. That is why she made a strict decision to follow all the rules and procedures that the government offered to her and to Rachel.

They were sent more and more new applications. The amount of paperwork was overwhelming, but she decided not to ask Herbert for help. She did not want him to know all her financial problems.

Della never asked Herbert for financial help or for additional cash. Never ever! She was grateful for everything Herbert offered. She felt and she knew that Herbert appreciated this. But this dance between her status as a low income refugee and the status of a woman with a rich American man made her very tense and confused. She did not always know how to behave with people who appeared in her life. With some she kept her mouth shut and did not tell them a word about Herbert and her good fortune; with others she did not want to look like a poor helpless refugee from the Soviet Union. It felt like she was dancing on a tightrope. Being an honest person by nature, Della was not happy with this duality in her life, but reality made its corrections.

She remembered a wise Japanese saying: "Excessive honesty borders on foolishness." One of her new woman-friends offered Della this advice: *"Never tell a lie; never tell the whole truth* . . .and *never pass up a public restroom."*

Laughing at herself, she understood that *"Never tell a lie; never tell the whole truth"* should become the main principle she must follow at this period of her American life. And, Della chuckled to herself, never passing up a public restroom was probably good advice, too.

At home, Rachel spent most of her time in bed as a helpless invalid, all the time asking Della for help. Della felt like Rachel's servant. But as soon as Herbert appeared in their apartment, Rachel forgot all about her aches and pains. She changed from her robe to a house dress. Then the walker appeared in the bedroom doorway, followed by Rachel in her best dressing gown, with her hair thoroughly brushed.

One evening Rachel demanded Della give her lipstick. Della gave Rachel her own tube of lipstick, a little bit used. Rachel critically looked at it and was not satisfied.

"You could buy me a new one."

"What color do you want?" Della laughed.

"Very beautiful."

"Good."

From then on when Herbert came to visit, Rachel's lips shone with brand new lipstick.

Usually Rachel came into the living room with a standard excuse.

"I will quietly watch TV. I will not bother you."

Did You Ever Have the Chance to Marry an American Multimillionaire?

She sat in the corner of the sofa, took the remote control, and put on the TV. Because she didn't hear well, the sound of the TV was so loud that Della and Herbert had to increase the volume of their own voices.

"When will we eat?" Rachel asked.

"Are you hungry? You ate recently."

"I would love to have a bite."

"What do you want?"

"You have a guest at home. Are you going to invite him to eat? You must! It is your obligation as a hostess. Let us sit at the table and I will eat whatever you give me."

Herbert never refused to eat homemade food. At the table Rachel showed her liveliness. She participated in the conversation and discussed all her problems with Herbert. Della was the translator.

When Herbert came, Rachel was always around and witnessed all of Herbert's and Della's movements. Herbert did not like it. Della did not like it either, but said to him, laughing, "Don't pay attention, she is an old woman; she has nothing in life more interesting than us."

Obviously Della needed to take some action about Rachel, but she was too busy. She had a lot of other stuff on her plate to take care of. Plus studying English in college required enormous homework to do. It was all too much.

CHAPTER 26

Herbert often picked up Della at the college and took her to lunch. Della couldn't help but notice that for driving her to welfare appointments he always took his old car, but to the college he drove his beautiful, brand new white Lincoln and opened the door of his luxury car for her. Della did not like this showing off. The students, her friends, were around, mostly young people who just recently came to America from all over the world. They drove very modest cars or did not have a car at all and waited for the bus.

Herbert's new luxury car was not appropriate in this situation, and she told this to him many times. But he did not care; he liked to play an American wizard.

Herbert usually took her to one of two restaurants: Bali Hai on Shelter Island, or Tom Ham's Light House, one of the best seafood restaurants on Harbor Island. Both of these places had a spectacular view and served delicious buffets for a very reasonable price.

After lunch they walked near the bay. Della looked at the shining water of the bay, the tall beautiful buildings in downtown San Diego across the bay, and couldn't turn away her eyes from this beauty.

"Is it real or it is my dream? Am I really here in America?" again and again Della asked herself. "I cannot believe it. Is it my imagination? No, I know, it is real. Yes, yes, definitely it is real. But I do not feel that it is real. I don't! What is going on with me?"

She touched the trees, bushes, breathed in the fresh air, closed and opened her eyes, and still she did not feel that she was there.

"What is wrong with me?" she asked herself. There was no answer. She repeated this question many times, many days, many nights. Too much was going in her mind. She often awoke at night, trying to explain to herself that everything that she felt was just simply an adjustment of her mind and body to a new environment. She tried hard to convince herself,

Did You Ever Have the Chance to Marry an American Multimillionaire?

very hard, but she couldn't. This state of her mind bothered Della terribly, but she was not able to help herself.

Della felt like a passenger on an unknown train that was rushing her somewhere. Everything that happened and was around her in America she saw as if it flashed outside the window of this racing train. America was a reality for her and not real at the same time. It was impossible to explain. She was here and was not here. Yes, she could see the streets with English names, people speaking in English, she could touch everything, she talked in English herself, and completely understood that she was in the United States of America. But deep inside she had not embodied this.

Very often Della asked Herbert: "Am I in America?" "Yes, you are." Again and again she repeated the same question: "Am I in America?"

"Yes, yes, yes, my dear, you are in real America. Don't worry, my darling, you are here and I am an American and I love you so much."

Later she read an article in a Russian magazine titled "Have I Arrived Already in America?" A woman who lived in the United States for a year and a half wrote it. She still didn't believe that she was here, on this American land.

Other immigrants who lived in the United States many years told Della that they had experienced the same feelings. They said that it took from five to seven years to pass to have an inner feeling that America was their home. It occurred to Della that maybe that is why an immigrant cannot apply for citizenship until they've lived five years in the United States.

Even after living in America for five or more years, Della still felt conflicted. Looking back on her first steps in America, she realized how difficult coming to a new country actually was. She realized that our mentality is very conservative; how much it resists change. Somebody told her about the situation with their son: "We can take the boy out of the country, but we cannot take the country out of the boy."

A few years later it "seemed" to Della that maybe she really lived in America. And to be honest, sometimes she still was not sure.

CHAPTER 27

Herbert invited Della to Las Vegas.

"I cannot go, I am sorry. Somebody should be with Rachel," Della said.

"My housekeeper can stay with her."

"But she is Mexican. She doesn't speak Russian."

"So, find a Russian woman; is it a problem?"

Della did. She found a Russian woman who agreed to stay for a few days with Rachel.

In the early morning the beautiful white Lincoln waited for Della near her gate. She came out from the building feeling like Cinderella to whom the Fairy sent this magic white carriage with a wonderful Prince sitting inside.

"Good morning, my Princess!" Herbert said.

"Good morning, my King!" Della kissed him.

"Welcome to the next higher step on your ladder of success in America! Belt yourself in and let's go!"

Herbert started the car. Della's fantastic Carriage ran fast in the early morning's empty city. She opened the window letting air with aroma of all the pine and palm trees fill their lungs and their car. Herbert drove fast. Three hours later they stopped in a little town named Barstow for lunch.

"I always take a rest here. This town is still in California, but we are approaching Nevada. It will be hot. You will enjoy watching Nevada's desert. You will like it a lot!"

Absorbing the vast desert with its stony mountains fringed with a blue sky above, Della whispered to herself: "Thank you, God, thank you, thank you. Bless America! Bless me! Bless Herbert."

They arrived in Las Vegas, and drove up to the Tropicana Hotel.

"I always stay in this hotel," Herbert said. "The manager of this hotel is my friend. He knows that my wife died and I am coming with you. He invited us at 4 p.m. for a cup of coffee."

Did You Ever Have the Chance to Marry an American Multimillionaire?

For the first time in her life Della entered a real casino with its specific sound of clanging coins. Between the flashing lights of the slot machines and the constant sounds of winning coins, it seemed like the casino was showering people with money. As they walked through the casino, she looked and looked, marveling that people's fantasies were really unlimited in designing these machines.

Each machine silently tempted and challenged newcomers: "Try me! I hide in myself so many opportunities for you! Try me! Try me! Try!"

Herbert gave Della $100:

"You play while I register, then I'll come after you and we will go to the room."

To put a $100 bill into a machine? These machines act like monsters, they grab money. No way was Della about to give a $100 bill to a machine! Instead, she put the $100 bill in her wallet.

"Stay here, this is a much safer place!" she told the $100 bill.

There was a big line to register. Waiting, Herbert tried a machine. Della watched. He played Poker on a dollar machine.

"Why are you not playing?" he asked.

"I do not know Poker."

"Go to a different machine, have fun!"

Della was excited to play, but she definitively did not want to change the $100 bill and put money into the machine.

"This $100 bill is my souvenir from Las Vegas. I will keep it," Della said. "You play on your dollar machines, I want to find something cheaper."

He took her to a 25 cents machine, put money in, and asked her to push the "spin" button. Feeling somehow afraid, she put her finger on the button and pushed. Everything on the screen started to dance and make noises. Della watched it with an open mouth. She won! The machine gave her 37 free spins! With her first try! Now the machine did its own spinning over and over. With every turn a new picture or a face appeared, like in an animated movie. The result: the first time she tried this gambling fun in the casino she won $84 with a 25-cent investment. The Tropicana casino certainly welcomed Della. Excited, she again pushed the button. Nothing. Again, nothing. Della did not like it.

Herbert laughed: "This is how it goes with gambling. You win and lose. Lose and win. Mostly lose."

Some of her money was still left in her credit. "Oh, no, I will not give all my money away." She cashed out what was left.

"You want to continue to play, don't you? We came here for three days. Better be patient. Let us go to our room, change, and go upstairs to say 'Hi' to the manager."

The manager, a friendly, handsome young black man, welcomed Herbert and Della to Las Vegas. The meeting was brief. Afterwards, Herbert asked Della:

"Are you tired, Dellishka?'

"I am okay. What are your plans?"

"I drove enough today and prefer to relax. I ordered the tickets for a show named *Jubilee*. I want to excite you, my darling, to surprise you, and to make you feel in Seventh Heaven. You will be shocked. Ready?"

"Ready. But how about you? You drove a long way."

"Let us go to the room, take a shower, and rest for a little bit. We will have time for dinner and then we'll go to the show. It is one of the best shows in Las Vegas."

※

Jubilee... The topless beautiful girls appeared on the stage. Fabulous feathered headpieces embellished their heads. Della inhaled deeply. It was the most glamorous entertainment she ever saw in her life.

"Wow! I am thinking now: would it be possible in the Soviet Union, Herbertchik? Watching these girls, all Russian men would go nuts and immediately run for vodka."

The next day Herbert took her to another show: *David Copperfield.* Herbert definitely wanted to amaze Della. Three days in Las Vegas were like fireworks for Della. Beautiful hotels, fabulous meals, and endless

Did You Ever Have the Chance to Marry an American Multimillionaire?

fantasies to entertain people. Is Las Vegas a gorgeous city or a money-making carousel? Definitely both, and much more.

They were sitting in the booth waiting for the show to begin. Herbert looked upset.

"What happened, Herbertchick?" Della asked. "Anything wrong?"

"Yes. My son called me. The children decided to hire a lawyer to go through all our assets."

"Your son is a lawyer himself. Why do they need to invite anybody else?"

"He is one of the participants. They decided to have an independent lawyer."

"It is serious. Perhaps your children are right. What is the problem?? Let them do it."

"They put the case on the Probate. It can take a long time."

"Can you change it?"

"No, I cannot! Unfortunately! They are young, you are young. I am old. I do not want to waste my time. I want to finish it as soon as possible."

"Well, my darling, we are here now, in Las Vegas. You will worry about this tomorrow, at home. Let us enjoy the moment, please. Let us watch the show."

After the show they went to casino, but Della felt tired.

"Please, enough is enough. It is late. Let us go to our room." Della asked Herbert.

Next morning he wanted again to go somewhere. Della felt too overwhelmed.

"Herbertchik, thank you. It is too much for the first time. It is not easy to digest all of these at once. Shall we now go back to San Diego?"

Driving home, he told Della: "We will come here again and again. I used to come with my wife every two months. I like it here."

"Okay, darling. Please, do not drive so fast; we are not rushing anywhere."

"How about Rachel? She is waiting for you."

"The woman who is with her is very nice. I know her. Rachel is fine."

CHAPTER 28

YES, THE WOMAN was very nice, but she was almost in tears when Della came back.

"What happened?"

"Rachel yelled at me, behaved as a general and treated me like a soldier at fault. Whatever I did for her was wrong. I am so glad you are back. I am leaving immediately, and if later you need help with your aunt, find somebody else."

Della paid the woman, who hurriedly took her things and literally ran out of their apartment.

Rachel started to yell at Della:

"How did you dare to go away for three days and leave me alone with who knows whom?"

"Stop it, Rachel, immediately. Go to your room."

"I do not want to go to my room. I am hungry! Give me something to eat!" Rachel demanded. Della said quietly with iron in her voice:

"Go to your room! Right now! Shut the door and sit there! Without a squawk!"

Herbert was watching this ugly scene.

"Forgive me, Herbert, and forgive her. She became too old. I cannot handle her anymore. I have the telephone of a facility for elder people with a Russian owner. I will call there right now."

"Dellishka, do not be mad at Rachel. She is just really old. I will go home, take a shower and rest, then will come back later and we will go for dinner. Do not prepare anything, just something for Rachel. You also rest, darling. It was a long ride."

Herbert left.

The next day the Russian owner of the facility for elderly people came to see Rachel. She looked at Rachel who was asleep in her room.

"My facility is private. It is a house with six rooms and a pool. Each room is separate. Some of the clients sit in their wheelchairs near the pool, they love it. All rooms are taken. All my six clients are Americans, but it doesn't matter. They are old, they do not communicate with each other. One woman is terminally ill. The doctor said that she is close to her end. Maybe a month, maybe 6 weeks. You need to wait, or to find another place for your aunt.

"I am the owner of this place, but I am not always there. A Russian couple, man and wife, help me. They do all the cooking, cleaning, etc. They bathe the clients, give them medications, comb them, and so on. Rachel will be able to communicate with them."

"I will wait, I cannot find another place with Russian-speaking caregivers. But I need to see your house and the room. Can I come tomorrow?" Della asked.

The next day Herbert drove her to this house. It was in a nice location, clean, and the room was very cozy. Rachel would be next to the pool and have a blooming tree outside her window.

They discussed the price. The owner did not accept any insurance, and Rachel's pension was not enough to pay for the room and everything else. Della must pay additional cash for Rachel and she was not able to do it.

"I will pay the rest!" Herbert said. "You need to be free, Dellishka, enough Rachel on your shoulders."

Herbert paid the deposit and they left.

Della did not know how to express her gratitude to Herbert for his emotional and financial support. She asked herself: *Did it really come from Herbert?* Somehow deep inside, Della believed that this kaleidoscope of

Did You Ever Have the Chance to Marry an American Multimillionaire?

good things that life poured onto her in America really came to her as a reward for her unpleasant past.

Did God send Herbert to her as compensation for her suffering in the Soviet Union? Who knows? If so, thank you, God! Thank you, America!

Life whirled Della in a continuous vortex of new events and challenges. Oh, it was so strenuous to handle and to digest everything that came into her field of attention. She was so happy and, at the same time, so overwhelmed. She shared her feelings with friends.

And what did Della discover? Not all her dear people were happy for her when she was feeling euphoric. A black web of envy started to grow deep inside of their souls, but Della learned this much later.

What Della learned was that these friends could hide their true feelings for a while, but someday there would be a burst of this concealed jealousy. And when it happened, it would be like a volcano exploding hot lava of dirty gossip and hatred all over her.

She wasn't prepared for this the first time it happened, but after that she told herself to be ready for it, and to try to avoid this situation. It was painful for Della to watch how her recent best friends opened their snake faces.

People's envy! It is an eternal, unending, timeless phenomenon. Nothing is truly learned until it is lived.

CHAPTER 29

GORGEOUS SUMMER APPROACHED San Diego. They came to the restaurant "Kona Kai" for a lunch. A sparkling water surface of a beautiful bay shone in front of their eyes. Gorgeous white boats and yachts rocked on the waves and waved to Della and Herbert with their sails.

Herbert took Della's hands, put them on his clean shaven face: "I feel with you in Heaven. I want to talk about something serious. On June 15, 1993 will be a year since my wife died. Our property was evenly divided between us; 50% belongs to me, 50% belonged to her. She left her 50% to her three children. I would love my part of the property to be legally separated from the children. An attorney works at probate now and it will take a few months. Thinking about my future, I am trying to make plans, and my plans cannot be without you. Our relationship is very important to me. I am taking it very seriously and I am dreaming to marry you, if you are willing to be my wife." Herbert gave Della a nice card with a sign: "To My Wife" and added "to be."

Did You Ever Have the Chance to Marry an American Multimillionaire?

Della became very quiet. She did not say anything.

"Why don't you tell me anything?" he asked.

"I do not know what to say. Is it a proposal?"

"No, not yet, it is just my thoughts about us in the nearest future. I need to be financially independent to be ready for marriage."

"Herbertchik, it is very serious. I came to America as a Jewish refugee from the Soviet Union. I am legally here and America supports me. If I marry you, I will lose all the benefits America gives me as a refugee. Perhaps you know and understand this. Now I have my pension, it is very small, but it is my money and I will have that money for the rest of my life. If I am your wife, I will totally depend on what you would give to me. I cannot totally depend on you, it will be wrong."

"Do not worry, it is not a problem, and it is not what we should talk about right now."

"Perhaps... but I would feel comfortable only being protected in our marriage. Life is life. Any situation can happen."

"My children love you very much. They will be glad if I marry you."

"Oh, Herbert, money can be a big issue. Just remember this when you plan to marry me, a poor refugee from the Soviet Union."

"Let us not talk about this right now, Dellishka. You will have more than enough!"

"I do have already enough, Herbert, and do not want to lose it. No need to talk about this now, but I am glad that I told you my situation. So, you see us as husband and wife, living together, don't you?"

"Yes; it feels so good. Very warm feelings."

"I just recently have read somewhere: 'Husband and Wife are like hands and eyes. When hands are in pain, the eyes cry. When the eyes are crying, the hands wipe the tears.' A very nice and touching expression."

The waiter brought the food. Herbert raised his wine glass:

"To us, my darling!"

"To us!" Della whispered.

Look at this exotic picture! A mature couple rides an elephant!

Del Mar Fair in San Diego offered this fun.

Herbert didn't want to do it. Della teased him:

"Let us go!"

"Oh, no, no! Not me," he said. "If you want, go ahead, have fun. I'll watch you."

Della was not comfortable doing it alone. But her curiosity overcame her fear. With the help of the worker, she hoisted herself onto the elephant's back, feeling its boundless, warm, heavy body covered with short bristles. The animal peacefully breathed under Della and didn't care at all who sat on his back, ready to start his routine ride.

"Come on! Quick! Let us have fun!" Della waved to Herbert.

Now, seeing Della on the elephant, he couldn't resist. In his youth he rode horses and got many awards for this. Herbert climbed up with a youthful vigor, and sat behind Della. They both felt that they had straddled a living mountain.

The elephant showed no interest in them. For him they were two little nothings on his back. He was bored with the many people around and submissively continued his sluggish march.

Did You Ever Have the Chance to Marry an American Multimillionaire?

But for Della and Herbert, riding the elephant was really an unusual experience. Excited, Herbert turned her face to him, kissing her every minute.

"Stop it!" she laughed. "I will fall off the elephant!"

"Never! I will not let you. I am holding you and will hold you always!"

They had a wonderful day at the fair.

Herbert brought her home to rest and left. He came back later, all dressed up.

"You look so festive! What happened? Anything special?" Della asked.

"Yes! Come to me."

Herbert sat her in the armchair, took her hand, and put a beautiful diamond ring on her finger.

"It is not just a ring. It is an engagement ring. I will do everything to make you happy. I will be always near and always for you, my love. I promise and I swear."

CHAPTER 30

Herbert really liked to have fun. He usually looked in the newspaper to find a place to get some joy. Once he asked Della:

"Would you like to participate in a dinner theater?"

"What do you mean?"

"It will be a regular dinner. But the restaurant wants to attract more guests. They offer a jocular performance. They will make this dinner as if it is a *"Wedding with a Killing"*. They will invite five professional actors to play the main roles: the bride, the groom, and the closest relatives. People who would like to come to this dinner are expected to play the guests of the 'wedding'."

"It might be fun. Let us do it," Della said.

Herbert sent them the payment for the dinner; they called him and asked for his and Della's age and what they looked like. Taking these details into consideration, they assigned the roles between all the participants. Then they sent a huge package with the script, the roles of the main actors, and the roles of other guests.

The topic of the story was funny. The Groom, a very rich young man, was the owner of property in the most privileged areas in San Diego—Coronado and La Jolla. The Bride wanted to snatch these two appetizing pieces from him and hired a lawyer for this purpose. The Groom intended to sell this property to protect himself from very aggressive inducements of his future wife. He asked his Aunt Rosa, who was an experienced real estate broker, to find a good buyer.

The Lawyer, a reckless gambler, secretly went to Las Vegas and lost both of these rich pieces of property. Certainly, the Groom and the Bride did not know about this. Herbert and Della were supposed to play very important guests (VIP) at that wedding. Herbert was assigned the role of this Lawyer, and Della got the role of Aunt Rosa.

Did You Ever Have the Chance to Marry an American Multimillionaire?

The rules required that all participants to be in their roles when they approached the restaurant, to behave and to talk as if they came to a real wedding. Della was in a gorgeous dress. Across her chest she put a huge slogan:

For Sale: Coronado, La Jolla, and Russia

They came to the restaurant. Everybody introduced themselves by the names of their roles. It was so much fun to watch those adults seriously playing this game. Herbert—the Lawyer, who was a gambler and also liked to be drunk, walked a bit shakily. Della—Aunt Rosa, walked around with her head proudly lifted and looked at everybody with piercing eyes. All the guests took their assigned places at the tables. The Bride in her beautiful white wedding dress immediately attacked the Groom, demanding La Jolla and Coronado. The Groom resisted. The Bride started to talk loudly, threatening the Groom. The Groom tried to calm down her aggressive behavior. They played out an ugly scandal.

Suddenly Della, who played Aunt Rosa, got up, came out from her table to the stage, stood up in front of the Bride and all of the guests and "relatives", pointed her finger in the Bride's face and told her how dishonest this Bride was.

"I know the groom, my nephew, since he was born. He is a very nice man. You want to marry him only because of his money, and I, his Aunt Rosa, would not permit this wedding and will not let the Groom, my lovely boy, be robbed by you, the so-called Bride, a terrible rascal in an expensive white wedding dress that my nephew lovingly bought for you! No way! This wedding is a fiction!!!"

Everybody was shocked. To jump out from the table was not in the Aunt Rosa's role. Della's unscripted speech in the middle of the stage destroyed the planned scenario. Everybody understood this and started to play their role more actively according to the new circumstances, adding their own details. The play became really alive; nobody knew how it would go forward, even the main actors. Funny, but the rest of the participants who were sitting indifferently just waiting for the dinner to be served became active, too.

The Lawyer (Herbert) also got up and stated firmly to the Bride that due to these new circumstances, he must increase twice the money the Bride should pay to him to get La Jolla and Coronado from the Groom (even though he had already lost these properties in Las Vegas, but certainly, it was his big secret.)

The flare of emotions reached their apogee! Suddenly there was a noise of a shot and the Bride fell 'dead'. All the guests participated in the investigation: Who killed the Bride? Finally, the "killer" was found. The play was over and the restaurant announced that dinner was ready to be served.

The "killed" Bride—a professional actress—got up from the floor, ran over to Della, and began kissing and hugging her.

"You made the play tremendously alive! How did you decide to do this?" the Bride asked Della. Della kept repeating: "I do not know. I just jumped in. I really cannot explain it." Della was rewarded with the best praise: a bottle of Champagne, plus the title The Best Actress in the Show, plus a free dinner. They credited back money to Herbert. People finished their dinner, but did not want to leave. Two hours ago they came to this place as total strangers, and now they talked as if they had known each other for ages. Della and Herbert met June and Jerry that evening. After this dinner they kept a very warm friendship.

Meeting June brought a new stream of interests into Della's life. She introduced Della to "The San Diego Senior Stage Academy" directed by talented Jack Bunning. Both of them, June and Della, participated in numerous performances that were given at the San Diego Old Globe Theater and other theaters. It was a wonderful life experience that lasted several years. At that time, Della's journalistic hobby helped her to write many stories, amazingly in English. She read her own stories from the stage of the Old Globe Theater and sang Russian songs. Della met there many great people who became her lifetime friends.

Did You Ever Have the Chance to Marry an American Multimillionaire?

This dinner that Herbert by chance found in the newspaper, opened to Della the taste of acting and curiosity for the stage behind the curtain. It became an unexpected turn in life. Della learned and learned and learned. Again and again, America opened for her new possibilities. Definitely, we never know what the next moment will bring to us.

CHAPTER 31

ONE YEAR OF Della's American life had passed. No, it did not pass, it ran away like crazy. Della even didn't have a chance to realize the unbelievable, incredible spin her days were evolving into.

"Stop, take a deep breath! Calm down!" she talked to herself very firmly, with all her inner power! It did not help. Her mind, also very firmly, refused to obey. Her mind declared its independence! Some power inside pushed her to act in an unstoppable whirl. It tremendously drained her, made her tense, and created more sleepless nights and restlessness.

She understood totally the stupidity of this inner rush. She knew that doctors and their pills wouldn't help her. She understood it back in the Soviet Union. It was a period in her life when she was very sick and bedridden. Pills made her mind foggy. No way. She needed a clear mind and ability to be focused. She needed energy. Della searched for any healthy source of energy, trying to watch what she ate. A juicer became her first helper. Fresh squeezed carrot and apple juices became a must to Della. Instead of pills, Della discovered for herself many interesting things: Yoga, meditations, good music, prayers, affirmations, walking in the park or the beach, connection with nature, etc.

She knew how important it was to choose the people who surrounded her. She learned to separate herself from people she did not feel comfortable with, to leave the movie she did not like, to avoid reading junk books, to not watch TV shows saturated with crime and blood. She watched news only very briefly or not at all, especially violent news.

In America, Della did not want to go again through tremendous tenseness. Things were going much easier in her life now. Soon Rachel would move to a wonderful place to live, and then a huge burden would be lifted from Della's shoulders. And, of course, she had Herbert's love and supportive hand.

Did You Ever Have the Chance to Marry an American Multimillionaire?

"Enjoy life! You deserve it!" Della repeated to herself. "Let only positive thinking enter your mind!"

◦⌒◦⌒◦

Herbert asked Della to move into his place:

"Find somebody to take care of Rachel for this month. Why should we waste a month of our life waiting for Rachel to be taken into the facility?" he said.

Della told Rachel that she was going to live with Herbert and cannot be anymore with her. Rachel's reaction was firm: "No, you cannot do it. I will not let you. I am old, I will not live long. When I die, then you can do whatever you wish."

Rachel really was sure that Della's only obligation was to take care of her. Della hugged her. "No, my dear. My life belongs to me, not to you. Try to understand. You will live as long as God lets you. I am not going to wait for your death. I found for you a wonderful place to live, it will be available in a month or so. I do not want you to die and do not want to wait for your death to live my life. You will live in a gorgeous place in a room near the pool; you will have much better care than I am able to give you. The money America gives to you is not enough to pay for it. Herbert is willing to pay the rest."

"I will not go anywhere!" Rachel declared.

"Do you love me, Rachel? I am also not young and not healthy. You know this. I do not have the strength to look after you. You know what I went through in my life. Herbert is God's gift to me. If you love me, please, take kindly what I prepared for you. I will not do anything bad to you. You know this."

CHAPTER 32

HERBERT'S STEPSON AL lived in Los Angeles. He was a lawyer in Beverly Hills and invited Della and Herbert to celebrate Thanksgiving. They spent a wonderful weekend with Al's family. While there, Herbert taught Della to play billiards. She had never played it before, and she had a lot of fun. Indeed Herbert knew how to entertain her.

Herbert continued to show Della gorgeous places. Christmas time was approaching. Driving around the city, they enjoyed beautiful sparkling decorations.

Herbert lived in a two-bedroom condo. Actually, it was a small separate cottage with one bedroom and a den, attached by one wall to another

Did You Ever Have the Chance to Marry an American Multimillionaire?

same-sized condo that belonged to his neighbors. It was built in the late sixties and its windows looked to the north. Herbert told Della that he and his wife had had a big house. When the children grew up and were gone, they bought this small condo which was located close to their business.

When Della visited him there for the first time, she thought that it looked like a dwelling of old fashioned people. It was very clean, almost sterile, but the sense was that everything was covered with a web. Definitely, there was not a glimmer of bright atmosphere in this condo.

Herbert's wife, a sick, old woman, was on her deathbed here during her last two years. An unhappy, choking mood still lingered. The furniture was old. It didn't look shabby, just old fashioned, maybe even antique. The bedroom set was dark brown from solid oak and looked heavy. A picture above the king-size bed represented a religious motif and was painted on black velvet in dark colors. There were two gorgeous lamps at each side of the huge bed. Each lamp represented a Yogi sitting in a Lotus posture. The lamps were black also. Why was everything decorated in black? Why lamps representing yogis?

"Did your wife practice yoga?"

"No, never."

"How about you?"

"Never."

"So, why do you have these lamps?"

"They are very peaceful."

"Yes, they are, and they are very beautiful and unusual."

Herbert rarely invited Della to his house. He preferred to spend time in her home. Della felt tired of Rachel's permanent presence, and her constant need for attention. Herbert lived across the street; they could spend some time privately in Herbert's house without Rachel's company. When he invited Della out, she asked him sometimes:

"Why should we run anywhere? Let us go to your place, you will light your fireplace and we will enjoy a quiet and peaceful evening."

He didn't like this idea. He didn't like to spend time in his home. He tried to be somewhere else.

When sometimes they came to his place for a short time and Della was waiting for him while he did something, she tried to imagine how she would live here. The condo was located in a nice green complex next to a swimming pool. It was a wonderful view to the blue water surface that sparkled with patches of sunlight reflection, and at nighttime was lit up with colored lanterns. The pool behind the bedroom's windows made the mood better. It was a pleasure to look outside of the windows, but the curtains always blocked the view. His condo was dark and gloomy. There seldom was sun inside.

Della opened the window to let fresh air inside and to see the greens and the pool. Herbert immediately closed the window and lowered the curtains back. She asked him why he did it.

"I don't want anybody to look in the window."

"Nobody can come close to the window because of the bushes."

"Oh, you don't know who can come closer. So many crazy people are around."

"So what if they look inside? What they will see? Your bed?"

"No, no, don't open the curtains."

She did not complain. It was not her home and not her business.

"But if you live here with him, will you be able to open the window?" flashed through Della's mind.

It was not easy to find a woman to live with Rachel. A few weeks passed. The room for Rachel in the Russian-owned facility was ready. To Della's surprise, it was not a big problem to persuade Rachel to go there. Rachel was smart enough to understand that it was inevitable. Of course, she complained, but not so much, and Della amazingly felt that Rachel liked her new place. It was a tremendous relief.

Finally Della belonged to herself. She wanted to be alone; she did not want anybody and anything to be around. No Rachel, no Herbert, no telephone calls, no English studying, no applications, no appointments. Nothing. Della's mind refused any activity. Just rest, rest, and more rest.

Did You Ever Have the Chance to Marry an American Multimillionaire?

She swam in the pool, enjoyed the Jacuzzi. She came back home, drew an aromatic bath, ate something tasty, and went to bed. She couldn't sleep, so she got up and drank chamomile tea. That didn't help. Take a sleeping pill? No, Della hated pills with their horrible after effects. She got up again, walked to the bathroom without any energy, and looked at herself in the mirror. She looked deep into her own eyes. She wanted to talk—not with her image—but with her soul.

"Finally you can take care of yourself. Can you? How many years did you take care of Rachel? She broke her hip in 1982... Today is 1994. 12 years? Plus lugging her to America. Is it over? Oh, no, it is not. For the rest of her life you will have the responsibility for her staying in the facility, to make payments, to take care for her health, etc. Isn't that enough Rachel in your life?

"What are you going to do now? You have a nice two-bedroom apartment. You have an American man who invited you to live with him. He loves you and offers you a lot. You are in America. Did you try to live with an American? Never? So, try it now! Go ahead, make a new step in your life.

"What to do with this apartment? To give it up? Really, why do you need this place? Why do you need all this furniture and all the things in it that you collected living in America? You are only two years in the USA, everything looks nice, you did a good job. You have everything and it is all yours. To throw it away and to depend on Herbert's bed or his pillow or his fork or spoon to eat? You pay rent here, silly to pay it if you have a free place to live with Herbert. Or maybe not silly. Your apartment is on a special program, the rent is affordable. As soon as you give up the apartment, you will lose the eligibility for the program; it will take years to get it back or maybe never. You do not know how you will feel in Herbert's condo. So??? What is your decision?"

Della continued to look deeply into her eyes in the mirror.

"It is late. Tomorrow is another day. Go to bed! And sleep!" she ordered herself.

After that, she slept peacefully. In the morning Herbert called.

"I tried to look at my house with your eyes. Perhaps we should change some things before you move in."

"Thank you, Herbertchik. Let us look together what can be done."

Herbert painted the condo in beautiful colors according to Della's taste. He replaced the old dark carpet with white carpet, and bought a new white bedroom set with a king bed. The bedroom shone. He did not want to change the furniture in the living room. "It is antique," he said.

Herbert was smart.

"I know that you are a bit scared how you will feel living in my place. I do not want to push you to do anything against your will. I want you to be comfortable with everything that we are doing. Keep your apartment for now. I will pay the rent. Do not worry."

A wave of appreciation arose in Della's heart. She moved into his condo. A new chapter in her life had begun.

CHAPTER 33

LIKE A NEW happily married couple, they ran throughout the city looking for everything to embellish their nest, changing bedding, towels, pictures on the walls, dishes, rearranging the kitchen, patio, taking out old stuff. On the patio they put gorgeous blooming roses and orchids. The condo became alive.

The old stuff Herbert had before was not so bad, and maybe very valuable, because many of the things in the house were antiques. Della did not care about antiquity. She held the firm opinion that anything in our life was supposed to be helpful, useful, but not old. Old stuff keeps somebody's old energy. We do not need anybody's old vibrations. Things around us are supposed to be changed so the current of life can flow freely. Della asked Herbert if he really wanted to keep and to use some of the so-called antique stuff.

"No, I would prefer new furniture and new other things, but some of my stuff is really expensive; it is silly just to throw it away."

"Some of your things look like they belong in a museum," Della said. "The antiques make us feel obligated to be very careful in using them and be somehow a part of an ancient ceremony."

Herbert asked if he could keep them in Della's apartment until they found a buyer. Della's place became storage for his antiques.

Finally Herbert's condo looked more or less cozy and Della moved in. Herbert showered Della with so much love and appreciation. She bathed in his love and she gave him so much peace. They both bathed in each other's love.

Usually in the morning he took Della to college, and went himself to his office. Together with his children he owned a big business center with a restaurant, dance club, beauty salon, and many other small businesses. Fifty percent of the ownership of this center belonged to his deceased wife. Now the three children divided the 50% among of themselves. Since Herbert held the remaining 50% of this partnership, he was the main owner of this center.

The dominant problem was the restaurant. It was not rented out for a couple of years. It needed a big reconstruction that required a lot of money. Nobody from the family wanted to invest this money. Herbert spent most of his time trying to find a proper renter but it was useless. The rent was large and the restaurant was in terrible shape. The restaurant became the main concern for Herbert and he talked about this continuously.

Della talked to him:

"I don't know anything about American business, but my common sense tells me: two years you kept the rent too high, nobody wants to take this place, especially since it is not in good condition. You are losing money stubbornly resisting lowering the rent. Month after month the restaurant is empty and you continue to lose money. Plus you are wasting your time and energy. Actually, it is not only your time, our time is wasted, instead of going somewhere for our honeymoon."

"Be patient, Dellishka, be patient."

Days flew. Usually Herbert picked Della up from college, and then had lunch together. He rushed back to his office and left her alone at home. She did her homework for college and tried to keep her new home neat and cozy. Herbert constantly repeated how he loved her. He was so happy, his life was established, everything was fine. For Herbert. How about Della? In Herbert's condo some blunt, stuffy, irrepressible force pushed her mind. Della found herself helplessly flattened on the very bottom of a deep pit, where unrelieved suffocation attacked her.

Did you ever notice a heavy atmosphere in the room or even in the house where somebody was sick for a long time? It is in the air, somewhere around you. You start to breathe heavier, something compresses your chest, you don't want to choke, and your smile disappears from

Did You Ever Have the Chance to Marry an American Multimillionaire?

your face. You want to open the windows and let the fresh air and sun come into the room or to leave as soon as possible, and not to be here anymore.

This uncomfortable feeling becomes worse if death had occurred here. Is this heavy spirit real? Does it exist independently of our sensitivity or it is only the product of our own mind? Maybe people who didn't know what had happened here before would never feel this heavy spirit in this room. Anyway, it is curious why so many people feel the same way in that situation. Really, what creates this lack of comfort?

Della did not feel good, and to her terrible disappointment, she understood why. There was bad energy in Herbert's house. She had this experience with bad energy before, back in Odessa. It made her very sick in Odessa; she became an invalid and almost died. It pushed her to be involved in spiritual studies. She knew about this sad reality with energy vibrations very well. She was aware that she would not be able to ignore this. Plus the walls of the living room in Herbert's condo were mirrored. The curtains at the windows were always down, Herbert did not like to pull them up. It was dark inside even on the sunny days, and she felt like she was in a mirrored cage when he kept the lights on. Della felt weak, tired, cold, without any energy, and couldn't sleep well.

"What to do about this?" Della asked herself. There were no answers. A strong power pushed her out from Herbert's condo. She took long walks and swam in the pool; it helped her. She felt better, but as soon she returned to his place, uncomfortable feelings came back and she couldn't get rid of them. She thought that the spirit of Herbert's wife could be still there and did not want Della to be around. Who knows?

Sometimes she came to her own apartment that was across the street, wanted to study or take a nap there but couldn't. Things Herbert brought from his place choked her.

Now Della understood why Herbert avoided spending evenings in his condo and preferred to come to Della, even though the presence of Rachel was not desirable. Herbert kept the housekeeper in the house; he did not want to be alone in his condo during the nights.

Della talked to herself: "Well... life is a road with green and red lights. Now once again a red light appeared. Just wait, be patient, think positively and optimistically."

All these affirmations did not help. Della couldn't sleep. They were lying in the bedroom in a brand new king bed.

"How long was your wife bedridden here?"

"Two years."

"Was she in this bedroom all these two years??"

"Yes."

"Did she die in this bedroom?"

"Yes."

"We cannot live here, Herbert. Her ill energy will kill us. Trust me, I know this stuff. We cannot live in my place either. Rachel's old energy is there. Rent something near the ocean and we will have blissful years ahead. Otherwise, we will sit in hell. It is very serious, Herbert."

"What are you talking about? This condo is paid in full. It is mortgage free. I do not pay anything here. Do you want to create a huge expense for me?"

"It is not about expense. It is about our health and happiness. You couldn't live here by yourself and you kept the housekeeper as a protector, as a bumper. Now you sent her away and I became your bumper. No, my dear, I am not willing to be in this role. You told me you have money. Nobody takes anything to heaven. You must decide what is more important for you: yourself, your health, your relationship with me or your money in the bank. By the way, you do not use your money. The bank uses it, not you. You are pleasing your bank with a big account. I will not live here in this condo. Period. Sooner or later I will leave."

"Impossible!"

The next day Herbert took Della out to a nice restaurant for dinner.

"You are worrying too much, my love. You are very superstitious. I would love to give you this."

He opened a jewelry box. Inside was a beautiful Star of David, covered with diamonds.

Did You Ever Have the Chance to Marry an American Multimillionaire?

"Christians wear a Cross to protect themselves from an evil eye, this will protect you, my darling Jewish lady." He put his gift around her neck.

"Thank you so much. It is gorgeous, Herbertchik. Hopefully it will work. If it protects me, I will protect you. I will try my best to clean the energy."

"Do not worry, Dellishka, you will never be sorry that you moved into my place. I would like to take you to Ronald Reagan's Library. You will be amazed. It is in California, not so far from San Diego."

The grandeur of Reagan's personality amazed Della. How was a man able to do so much in one lifetime? Impossible. No, it was possible. He did it. Herbert loved Las Vegas. He enjoyed going there. As soon as he had a few free days, they drove there. He always found great shows to entertain Della. He really knew how to make each day joyous.

Della's friends came from New York. Herbert took all of them to Palm Springs, and then to Palm Desert. He invited them into the Marriott Hotel. Behind the main building was a huge lake. The hotel's hall looked like a palace. The boat came into the middle of this palace, took people, and then cruised around in the big manmade lake. In the middle of the desert. Amazing.

CHAPTER 34

DELLA AND HERBERT were invited to San Francisco for a Russian 1995 New Year's Party. The Russian restaurant was located in a two-story building on the second floor. On the first floor was a Chinese store. The Russian New Year's party unfolded in front of an amazed Herbert. At 12 a.m., when the new year was announced, everybody made toasts, ate, and danced. One o'clock in the morning, 2 o'clock in the morning, 3 o'clock in the morning—people continued to eat, sing, and dance. At 4 o'clock in the morning the frightened owner of the Chinese store below the Russian restaurant appeared in front of the Russian orchestra and asked them to stop the music immediately. The intense dancing destroyed the ceiling of the Chinese store. People ran downstairs and saw that the ceiling of the Chinese store was ready to collapse.

The party was over. Herbert said he would remember it forever. They drove back to San Diego laughing at the situation that they almost broke the ceiling celebrating a New Year's Eve in the Russian way.

Della was sitting in the car and looked at him. A handsome respectful caring elderly gentleman courted her as a refined treasure, with grace and elegance. He made Della feel very special. She really felt loved and unique. It was a terrific feeling. People at the Russian party watched this American man who did not understand a word of Russian with admiration.

"I thank you, Herbert, for giving me the opportunity to feel myself as a queen. I felt it, I was in this position, you lifted me up, inspired me to feel myself on the very top, I was in the height of attention and admiration. Thank you for praising me so high."

"I am always for you, my darling Dellishka. You are a bright shiny sun for me, and I am just a little dull candle near you."

When a man raises his woman on a high level, it works magical wonders: everybody around feels that this woman deserves to be honored and starts to behave with her in the same manner. Many times they went

Did You Ever Have the Chance to Marry an American Multimillionaire?

somewhere and people who never saw Della before, especially men, looked at her with admiration. She felt like the first lady of the ball. If we feel loved, these vibrations spread around, create magnificent aura, and attract other admirers. People feel great in this aura. This is the magic and power of love.

1995 started its run. The holiday rush was over. They both were busy: Herbert with his business, Della in college studying English and computer skills. They came home to rest and to enjoy each other. Della wanted to let in fresh air and light, so she pulled up the curtains, opened the windows, and rushed to the kitchen to make something delicious for dinner.

When she came back from the kitchen, the windows were closed and curtains were down.

She put on the air-conditioner to get some air movement. In a few minutes Herbert turned it off.

"We talked about this already, Herbertchik. Why do you do this again?"

"It bothers me, I don't know why."

"Let us go to the doctor."

"No, this is not a reason to go to doctors. Let us see what we have for a dinner."

This happened every day. If Della tried to talk to him, he changed the subject. The fighting with Herbert about these windows and air-conditioning made her extremely tired; she did not want to complain and she did not know how to deal with this.

"Tell me, please, Herbertchik, what is the problem with opening the windows and the curtains? Why don't you want to let the light in? Is there anything wrong with you that you are not telling me?"

He whispered: "Yes, it bothers my eyes, I have a terrible headache."

"How about air-conditioning?"

"My ears."

She hugged him: "Please, let us go to the doctor."

"I am fine. I have my business to take care of."

"No, you have yourself to take care of! You! You! And only you!!! Period. Plus me. Otherwise I cannot be here. Please, understand. I cannot be without air and in a dark room, I feel myself in a cave."

"Calm down, Dellishka, everything is fine."

"No, Herbert, something is going on, and you do not want to tell me."

"Everything is fine," Herbert told her with iron in his voice.

Herbert was a man. He would never show a woman his weakness. Della knew this.

At night Herbert slept soundly near Della, but she couldn't sleep even with a sleeping pill. Bitter thoughts choked her.

"What should I do now? Rachel has good care. Finally I received the freedom that I hadn't had in years. I had been working all my life and now I do not need to work. A housekeeper comes regularly to clean. I can enjoy swimming in the heated pool, walking around, reading books, and indulging myself. So, do it! What is the problem?"

It all sounded very dull and boring. Herbert had his business; She was just a witness to it, not a participant. They did not share common friends. He almost did not have any, and not all her friends were acceptable for him because they pulled her into activities he didn't want to share.

Della felt a thick, sticky, impenetrable atmosphere around her especially when she was alone. His place choked her, she felt totally unprotected inside. She asked herself a thousand times:

"What is the matter with you? You are with such a great man. Why do you feel so oppressed? Every woman would be happy to be in your place."

With this heavy state of mind Della was losing all her power. She loved Herbert so much and yet she was unable to live with him. She became a prisoner and a slave of her attachment to Herbert. Sad thoughts and a sense of helplessness and defenselessness became the lurking robbers of her strength and the misery-making slumps in her health.

Della kept asking Herbert to change the house. There was a whole world out there for them to discover. He wasn't interested, and Della understood that he will always resist anything new in his life. Herbert was determined to keep her in his cocoon.

He felt that Della was bored and invited her for dinner out or to a movie. Some of their evenings had been enjoyable, but she was restless and tired of the monotony. Della had worked for too many years and now she was expected to sit home doing nothing, especially since she didn't drive and was tied up with Herbert. She felt under his total control.

"I am helpless without driving. I submitted my permit to DMV, it will expire in two months. I must learn to drive in two months. Am I able to do it? Impossible."

Herbert told her many times:

"You do not need to drive. You will be always able to call the taxi."

"Why do I need it? I can drive myself."

"It is dangerous to start to drive at your age."

"It was more dangerous, Herbert, to come to America at my age, but I made it and in addition brought Rachel, an old invalid."

Herbert definitely wanted her to depend on him. Something was wrong. He behaved differently now. Even with sex. He just enjoyed sleeping near Della, only hugging her and kissing her goodnight.

She understood he would not be happy if she started to do anything to get her driver's license. Della told herself: "Well, it is not his business, pay no attention to it." She lived in America for two and a half years; without him, she would be driving already and would have a car. Driving was a necessity for her sense of independence and convenience. And, she felt it would help Herbert.

CHAPTER 35

For two years Della studied in Mid-City College where she took different classes. Now she received an offer from Grossmont College. It was a higher level institution. They did not ask money from her, moreover they offered her a monthly grant. Della showed the letter to Herbert.

"Is it okay with you?"

"Why not? Certainly, take the classes. They will pay you money."

"It can be a problem. Grossmont is farther from your place, and the classes start at different times. How I will get there?"

"I will drive you."

"It will be a challenge for you."

"No challenges if it is for you, my Dellishka."

"Well, let us try."

Della took a very intensive course at Grossmont College. As Della predicted, Herbert was not always able to drive her and asked her to carpool with somebody. It was also a challenge.

The days were packed with duties for both of them. When the evening came, after dinner Herbert usually put TV on and, being tired, fell asleep near her. Della decided to cheer up their evenings.

"Herbertchik, you are too busy in business. I am with you, enjoy it."

"I do, Dellishka."

"Your mind is too deeply tuned to your tenants, to rent, etc. My head is busy with different topics. May I ask you something?"

"Whatever you want."

She asked him innocently:

"I heard that in America you have special stores for equipment to make sex."

Herbert looked at her with astonishment.

"Impossible. The government wouldn't permit it."

"Really? I thought it is a free country."

Did You Ever Have the Chance to Marry an American Multimillionaire?

"I don't know. You ask me shameful things. I never thought about this."

"Why do you take it so seriously? I am curious. Let us have fun. Let us find out. Why not?"

"I don't know even whom to ask about this."

"Do you still have Jacob's telephone number? He is a young man, he knows. He told me about this. Ask him."

"To ask Jacob? My old tenant? I cannot talk with my tenants about these things."

"Why not? You asked him to introduce you to me. I can ask him, if you do not want to."

"No, do not ask him. How can you or I talk with him about sex?"

"Easy. Or you think Jacob is sure that you don't make love to me and you don't know what sex means? It is not in your line. You are for him only a landlord. Landlords are too busy to make love."

"Of course not. I just don't want to discuss this subject with him."

"Herbertchik, I am teasing you."

"I know you are."

"May I continue to tease you?"

He laughed:

"Go ahead."

"You are American. Did you ever watch sexual movies?"

"What are you talking about? It is shameful. Of course, I didn't."

Della laughed. "Really? Never ever?"

"Never. I was married. Do you think that I could watch this disgrace with my wife?"

"With whom could you watch it, with a strange woman?"

"No, it was impossible."

"Why? You didn't have sex with your wife, did you?"

"Of course, we did, but what did I need this movie for? I had my wife, I had no need to watch these stupid movies."

"But you watch other stupid movies. You like to go to the cinema and you like TV."

"But these movies are about life."

"Sex movies are about death, aren't they?"

"I cannot argue with you. I was a busy man, I couldn't spend my time on foolish things."

"And now? Would you like to do some foolish things now? How about ordering a sex movie on TV?"

"Why do I need it now? I have you."

"I am from ignorant Russia. Would you like to increase my education in this field?"

"You are educated more than enough. You know everything."

"How do you know? Would you like to compare?"

Della teased him so much that finally he rented a sex movie. She watched him with curiosity. He was a unique American. At his age he saw a sexual movie for the first time in his life. Della spied on how his face was changing. He looked condescendingly. Then contempt arose in his face. Then interest appeared in his eyes. Then it was changed to exhilaration.

"Would you like a cup of tea?" Della asked him in the middle of the movie.

"Thank you. Not now. Later." He didn't want to be interrupted.

"How about an apple?"

His full attention was in the movie.

"No. Please, later."

"Why are you so excited? It is just a video. We can stop it and have a light snack. And then play it again."

"No. I want to watch it to the end and give it away. I don't want to keep it at home."

"If you don't want to watch it, you can stop the movie now and give it back. Why are you so nervous?"

"I am not nervous, I am curious."

"Are you not ashamed to watch this disgraceful movie in front of an intelligent lady and a foreigner? Shame on you. Look what they are doing on the screen. Stop it immediately."

"No, now I will watch it. And don't interrupt me, please."

Did You Ever Have the Chance to Marry an American Multimillionaire?

Della laughed almost to tears.

"You make me laugh too much," Della said wiping her eyes. "It causes wrinkles on my face. With you I need to discover unwrinkled laughter!"

Herbert laughed also.

Della replied:

"Okay, if you want to watch it, please do. But try to watch the movie very attentively. It is your educational process. Don't miss any single movement. Learn! Study!"

He laughed loudly.

"Herbertchik, please, forgive me for all this. I just want you not to be in business too much. And honestly, I am not interested in these sexual movies. It is not making love, it is sexual exercises they do to create the video. I agree, we do not need this."

"No, it is okay. It takes my mind off my job and makes me relaxed."

"I know. That is why I asked you to order it. It works for you like psychotherapy, isn't it?"

"Exactly."

After this he ordered the sex channel on TV and watched it very often.

"Why are you so interested in it?" she asked him.

"It really makes me relaxed."

"Maybe it is better to do it in reality?" she teased him again. He shook his head, laughing:

"You are something!"

"Of course, I am. Otherwise, I wouldn't be here."

"Yes, you are right. You are always right. You are my delight. I love you so much. I am so lucky to have you."

⊱✦⊰

Della made her firm decision to proceed with a driver's license. A friend introduced her to a driver instructor who could teach her to drive. Della met him and asked:

"My permit will expire in two months. Can you teach me how to pass my driver's license exam? First, I need to pass the exam in DMV, and after that I will take additional lessons with you to learn really to drive."

"We need to do it each morning, at 6 AM, when the freeway and the streets are empty. At least for two hours. Tomorrow I will come to your place at 6 AM."

As Della predicted, Herbert was very disappointed.

"It is okay, Herbert. I am also not happy with your closed windows, so what?" Della replied.

In a month and a half she got her driver's license. She was so proud of herself.

An intensive course at Grossmont College, driving lessons in the early morning, and sleepless nights made her extremely tense and exhausted. She desperately needed a rest.

Herbert again offered her Las Vegas. No, she did not want to go. She had become tired of Las Vegas.

"Herbertchik, let us go to New York for a week. I have wonderful friends there. The spring is coming. It is beautiful there in May."

"No, I cannot. I do not fly."

"What do you mean?"

"Very simply. I do not fly. When I was young, I was in a plane crash and since then I am afraid to fly."

"You never told me."

"You never asked."

"Are you serious?"

"Yes, very much. My wife wanted to go to Israel and she never did because of this."

"So, it means that we won't be able to go anywhere? I am waiting for my citizenship and for my passport. I am desperate to see the world."

"No, not me."

"Ridiculous. If you did not fly, why couldn't your wife go to Israel with a friend or with her children?"

Did You Ever Have the Chance to Marry an American Multimillionaire?

"What do you mean? Her husband is not flying and she will travel by herself?"

"But it was your problem, not hers. If you are in a car accident, will you give up your driving license forever? It is only psychological. You can get rid of this with good professional therapy in a few weeks. You never went to Europe, did you? Or to Hawaii?"

"Never."

"And your wife?"

"Never."

"It was very selfish of you. I lived all my life in the Soviet Union, behind the iron curtain, where I was not able to go anywhere, and now you want me to be stuck here because you have this twist in your mind? How can you demand this from a woman if you love her?"

"If we love each other, we enjoy being with each other and we do not need anything more."

"Herbertchik, you created a very comfortable philosophy. For yourself. No, darling, you put your woman in your own prison, using her love to you. I am surprised that your wife agreed with you. You limited your own life, but is it right to limit the life of your dearest person?"

"I cannot stay alone here."

"I told you, change the condo. Have you lived here for 25 years? It is time to move to a more gorgeous place. You cannot stay alone here? I won't do it as well. I cannot live in darkness. You do not want to open the curtains, please, let light come from the ceiling. Let us put the solar tubular above the table in the living room. I have an advertisement."

"But it is expensive."

"Ask how much. Here is the telephone."

Herbert resisted, but finally agreed and put a solar tubular in the roof of the living room and in the kitchen.

"By the way, Herbert, if you do not want to fly, let us make New York in a different way. Let us go by car and by train across the country. It will be great. So much fun."

"No, I cannot. It will be a long trip. I need to rent out the restaurant."

"But you have tried to do it now for a year. We can do this trip in two weeks."

"A good client can appear tomorrow. You cannot miss the chance."

"Whatever you say, dear. I am going to New York. My decision is firm. End of discussion."

Della watched Herbert. Usually a generous man, now he carefully counted the money he spent. In the morning he opened the newspaper and looked for coupons. He usually found coupons "Two for $3" for the International House of Pancakes and invited Della to eat breakfast there.

"Let me prepare breakfast myself, Herbert."

"Let us go out, Dellishka."

"Okay, let us go to the beach and eat there."

"No, it is too far away, and too hot and too much sun. These pancakes are around the corner."

Now he chose the cheapest stores and restaurants. The food was not good for Della and she wanted to cook herself. He didn't want to eat at home. For him to go out was a little relief for his occupied mind. Everything he bought was from the cheapest store. It didn't matter whether it was food or other merchandise. Della forgot when the last time was that they had fun.

Della looked at Herbert. Something was in his eyes that she did not like. Finally she decided to call Clint, Herbert's stepson.

"Clint, I noticed something different in Herbert's behavior. Something is wrong with him, but he doesn't want to tell me. Did you notice anything?"

"Yes, I did. I asked him to go to the doctor. He doesn't want to talk about this."

"He needs help. I do not know what to do. I feel terrible near him, I feel sick, without energy. I am taking now a very complicated course at Grossmont College. I am not able to do it and perhaps, I will give it up. Convince him to go to the doctor, or to go for a big vacation. He doesn't fly, but a good cruise will be helpful. You know him better."

Did You Ever Have the Chance to Marry an American Multimillionaire?

"I will talk to him again, Della, but he doesn't listen to me. Did he tell you that I broke with him?"

"Yes, he did. But health is more important. Please, talk to him. You can tell him that I called you. I am worrying and am asking you to talk to him."

"I will try."

"Thank you, dear Clint."

CHAPTER 36

Herbert and Della continued their routine life. On Fridays they often went to Temple Emmanuel for Sabbath. The service was in English but they used a lot of Hebrew. Della was not able to follow it. She never studied Jewish traditions. But Herbert liked Sabbath services.

They did a lot of things, but the happiness disappeared, evaporated, they were two humans that tried to keep together something broken.

Herbert spent all his working time at the business center, came home tired, and after dinner usually slept near the TV. At night he was also tired and had no desire for sex. He usually found a reason to say: "Sorry, Dellishka, we will do it tomorrow, not today."

Della tried to make him active, but he was not able to do anything.

After his recurrent failure Della told him: "I am sure you can feel like a young man. The modern medicine invented so many ways to extend man's potentialities, especially in America. An advice with a good doctor won't kill you. Maybe it is very simple to help you."

At that time Della didn't know about Viagra. Herbert, perhaps, didn't know about it also.

"What do you want from me? Do you think I am a machine? I don't remember when I was so active. I am great. I am proud of myself. I never had this experience with my wife. Today I was tired, two weeks later I will make you happy again."

"Two weeks later? Thank you very much for your sweet promise!"

"My wife told me that once in two to three weeks is good enough. It is normal."

"What should I do with you? An 80-year-old woman is a great authority on sex. Your wife was a good woman with all the beliefs of her time. You are here, in a new time, move forward, please."

"Be patient, it will come."

Did You Ever Have the Chance to Marry an American Multimillionaire?

"If you ask me, I will be patient and only for you, my dear. You deserve this. I hope it will come when I will be less than ninety. How old will you be? Let us set up a record. We can be in the Guinness World Records. We will repeat the Sara and Abraham story from the Bible. I will have a baby when I am ninety. Why not?"

"You ninety? Never ever. You are a woman without age. With your energy, you will live to be thousand years old, and still you will behave like sixteen."

Della laughed.

"Listen, you saw on TV that a furious girl cut the penis from her boyfriend and it was sewed back onto the man. Really, the United States is a terrific country. Here doctors can do everything. To change the gender is nothing for American doctors. How can they go about to make from a dummy a genius? It is so simple, just take out the stupid brains and put in instead smart ones. If it is possible to change the old heart, the main organ and engine of our body, and implant a young one, why can't they take off the old penis and exchange it for a great strong energetic new one? What do you think about this, Herbertchik?"

He roared with laughter.

"No, I am serious. Really, what is a penis? Certainly, it is an important tool, but compared to the heart it is secondary. This surgery would be cheaper than with the heart. Maybe Medicare would cover it. Or you can afford it anyway. Just try. Why not? You will be famous; all newspapers will shout out about you."

Della's fantasy became wild.

"Listen, because it would be a unique case, you can bargain with them and they can give you a special offer, for example, two for one. While one penis will be in use, the second will rest and can be held in a container with a special solution and nutrition to keep its energy balance, and, of course, with Parisian perfume to make it more attractive. You should ask them to make these penises interchangeable, with zippers."

Herbert was choking with laughter and almost fell off the bed.

Della continued:

"We can also order different sizes and they can be adjustable. You will become a young boy, your hair will grow again on your head and beautiful sixteen-years-old girls will stand in line to have an affair with you."

Herbert shouted with laughter:

"So, I won't need you anymore, in this case. I will trade you for two twenty year old!"

"Oh, here I will remind myself your advice: 'Be patient, it will come.' I would be very patient waiting for my turn to spend a night with you. No, really, let us change your penis. You will be the most famous man in the world. If you pay good price, they will find you a huge one and you will be a super man! I think that to do justice for my great ideas you should make me the first lady of honor in your harem."

"Don't worry. I will give you special permission to attend to my super penis whenever you want."

"Thank you, sweetie, you are so kind. Now I am not worried for my future."

Della couldn't stop.

"We will invent special nozzles for the penis. For Jewish men they will be different. Maybe, we will make it like special attachments to condoms. You know that I am an engineer, I need to keep my mind busy. I will work in this direction. We will discover something unbelievable. We will take out a patent for it and sell it wholesale and retail. We will create colorful labels on these nozzles and will rent them out. No, I am wrong, what I am talking about? They must be disposable like syringes. I should search in this field; maybe I can improve upon the best inventions that were done already. You should take me to the X-RATED F-STREET store; ask your tenants where it is located. Don't be afraid, you will gain a big respect from them because you would be interested in such things. They will pay more rent to you, to their landlord with such a developing personality. We will make a great business and expand it to Russia. The market for these things is unlimited there, especially if the label would be: "Made in USA." Women would be crazy about this and push their husbands to buy it."

Did You Ever Have the Chance to Marry an American Multimillionaire?

"You are really something. I will never be bored with you, my darling."
Della said:
"Okay, it is getting late, let us sleep."
"Thank you, Dellishka, you made me feel better with your jokes. Sweet dreams…"

She felt better also. A good joke is a great power. All desperate situations become nothing if you laugh it out. Laughter lights up the soul.

⁂

But later, at during another sleepless night, Della's head was occupied with endless thoughts.

"Why do I need these stupid jokes about men's penises? I feel like an idiot, a jerk. He doesn't want sex. He is afraid to do it or not able to.

"He doesn't fly; he will not go with me to New York. How could I leave him alone? I feel like a criminal. Why should I? He is not a child and I am not his babysitter. Go to New York! Get out from this condo!"

Herbert hired a Mexican woman Laila, who helped him in business and in the house.

"Herbert, can you ask Laila if she is willing to stay with you for one week? Please, let me fly to New York. I need it desperately. If Laila stays here you will be fine."

"My wife never left me alone."

"I am not your wife. Herbertchik, you demand too much from mw. I am very exhausted. I am not able to study now. I need to give up my classes and my grant at Grossmont. Unfortunately. Maybe New York will help. If you love me, please let me go just for a week. If you really care for me."

"Whatever you say, dear Della."

⁂

Herbert brought Della to the airport and gave her a neatly packed thick envelope.

"You have a long flight. Take a look at these papers."

"Okay, Herbertchik, I will. I hope I will become myself again in New York. I am sorry you will not be with me. I love you so much."

On the airplane Della opened Herbert's package:

"Prenuptial Agreement for Herbert Samson and Della Gordon."

Official paper created purposely for her. 35 pages. Each page defined Della's status in their upcoming marriage. "Separate" was the main word on each page, repeated many times. By this agreement nothing was given to Della Gordon. NOTHING! Moreover, there was a special note: the most expensive gift to her must be less than $200.

At the end of the agreement was the approximate estimated value of Mr. Samson's properties: $2.5 million dollars. There was another special note that this did not include everything Mr. Samson owned. He had more assets that would be added to the agreement later.

Della remembered that he once told her that he owns a big piece of land near San Diego. Also an enormously huge safe was in his garage. With his wife he owned four jewelry stores. When his wife became sick, they closed the jewelry business and perhaps all the valuables from these stores were kept in this safe.

The next page was prepared for Della Gordon. It was blank. On this page Della Gordon must declare the value of her assets and properties in the United States of America and other countries.

Della read this paper again and again and did not believe her own eyes. A man who every day assured Della that he loves her more than himself, that his love will last forever, showed her his fangs, his claws. Every word in that agreement declared that Mr. Samson is a king, an American King with money, with assets, with investments, with treasures, and Della is a destitute from the Soviet Union.

Was it a real official paper? Yes, it looked like it. It was signed by the lawyer with his name, address, and telephone number. Later Della called this number. Yes, it was a lawyer's office.

Della did not know what to do: to laugh or to cry. If Herbert gave her this paper, he was really mad at Della. Perhaps because she did not obey Herbert's rules.

Did You Ever Have the Chance to Marry an American Multimillionaire?

"Okay, Dellishka, for a few years you have had a millionaire near you. You did not realize it. Now it appears that he is not a millionaire, he is a big multimillionaire, because not everything that he owns is listed in this paper. Just put on the blank space under your name the amount of money you have in the bank, showing that you have nothing and sign the paper. You will be a multimillionaire's wife, poor as all the mice in the poorest churches because as his wife, you will lose even the small benefits the government pays to you."

Herbert was a person who collected things; he did not like to squander things. Recently Della had heard a joke: "The quickest way to double your money is to fold it over and to put it back in your pocket." It reminded her of Herbert's habit: he always kept his cash in the pocket, not in the wallet, folded over and tied up with an elastic band. After he paid for something he didn't miss the opportunity to count how much money was left. When she saw this she always caught herself in the thought that she never knows accurately how much money she has in her wallet. Maybe this is the reason that she is not a millionaire.

Yes, he was a collector, not a spender, who felt great having a large amount of money in the bank. When Della came together with Herbert to the bank, the manager of the bank jumped from his chair and accommodatingly looked at him. While Della stood in line to take care of her own account, Herbert was invited to a special room; he never went to the regular bank window.

Della asked him:

"Why does he jump around you?"

"Because I am a good customer."

"How much am I supposed to have in my account to be a good customer?" Della joked. Herbert laughed.

Later Della watched the face of the same manager when he talked with another customer. He looked at this client with impenetrable firm eyes. With Herbert he was a different person.

Herbert was very rich back in the fifties and sixties. He wanted to buy a beautiful house in La Jolla for about $300,000 (a lot of money at that time), but at that time Jews were not permitted to buy property in

La Jolla. He showed this house to Della. He told her that this house costs about 10 million dollars now. When Della met Herbert in 1992, his estate had become much larger. He and his wife owned four jewelry stores and a ranch with Arabian horses. His condo was full of prizes for the horses. They both, Herbert and his wife, were good riders. Actually, all Herbert's troubles began after his wife fell from a horse, broke her back, and became very sick. Plus later she had cancer.

They sold the ranch with Arabian horses. Certainly, everything that Herbert owned was invested somewhere. The bank was the main user of his money. His big house was sold when the children grew up. Della couldn't understand why they bought this two-bedroom condo, dark and small, with little windows always closed. Perhaps the reason was too simple: his wife being old and sick wanted a small place in which to spend her last years. But Herbert was fifteen years younger. Fifteen years are a big part of life. Why did he need to spend the rest of his life in such an unpleasant place? And why did Della need to be there?

Della bitterly sighed. He created not an agreement; he created a verdict. For whom was that verdict? For Della? No, he punished himself.

Herbert brought this agreement to Della when she flew to New York. Was it his revenge, his anger, his pain and weakness? No, Herbert was not like this. What was the real cause of creating this paper? Did the children push him to do this? No, he did not follow their advice. He usually made decisions himself. If he created this monstrous agreement it meant that he, himself, was in a very bad inner place. Was it a hope that Della, with her poor English, wouldn't understand the meaning of this agreement and sign it trusting Herbert entirely?

No, Herbert was not so naïve. He knew that Della would definitely read the paper. If he made a paper like this, it meant he was not able to control himself. What is going on with his mind, with his brain?

Della came back from New York. Herbert waited for her in the airport. He passionately hugged and kissed her.

"I missed you so much. I am so glad to see you. Let us go for dinner."

CHAPTER 37

They were sitting in a nice restaurant at Coronado beach.

"Tell me about New York."

"New York is New York, a grandiose city, the capital of the world. I met my friends; I was at the Statue of Liberty and at many other places."

"Did you have a chance to read the agreement, Dellishka?"

Della looked at Herbert, looked in his eyes, and laughed.

"Of course. I had this pleasure."

"Why are you laughing?"

"I understand I have a chance to become a wife of a multimillionaire."

"If you say so."

"When do you want us to be married?"

"As soon as you give me the signed paper, we will start to plan the wedding."

"Will I be in a white wedding dress?"

"Certainly."

"Who will pay for the dress?"

"I will, of course."

"No, you cannot."

"Why?"

"Because, according to the agreement, you will be allowed to give me a gift only for $200. The dress will cost much more."

"Do not worry about this. Do not pay attention what is written in this paper. This is a regular legal routine when people are going to be married. You just do not know the American laws."

Della burst out laughing.

"I should not pay attention to what is written in 35 pages?"

"Did you read all 35 pages?"

"Certainly."

"You are a genius, Dellishka. Forget about the 35 pages, just sign the first page under your name and we will be done with this."

Della laughed.

"My darling, you are a genius making me such an idiot. I am curious, how much did you pay your lawyer to create this masterpiece? Wasted money. We were happy when I lived in my place and you were in yours. We tried to live together. It did not work out. I am not going to marry you, dear. Never. Our marriage is a delusion, a soap bubble. I do not want to discuss any details. Let us enjoy our dinner."

"What are you going to do?" Herbert asked.

"What do you mean?"

"With your life?"

"What is the problem with my life? America generously supports me. I have my apartment. Thank God, I have my driver's license. I need a car, tomorrow I will call the person who taught me to drive. He will help me get a car."

"Are you mad at me, Dellishka? I love you very much."

"Better to love yourself, Herbert. Your condo is ghosted. It made you out of your mind if you created such a paper and asked me to sign it, not paying attention to what I am signing. I have learned that it takes years to build up the trust and only seconds to destroy it. You want to live in your condo and to become sick, go ahead! Do it! Without me. Your life is your life. But let me take care of my life. I am living in America for almost three years. Without you, I would already have a car, I would drive, I would be more protected.

You made me very upset, Herbert. I do not deserve it. I am not mad at you, I feel sorry for us, for you and for myself. You want me to depend on you totally, don't you?"

"Oh, no! I love you too much."

"Thank you. The paper you gave to me is real evidence of your love. Is it a revenge that I left you alone knowing that you are afraid to fly? You have this fear; deal with it yourself, without me. You are afraid to live in your condo alone. Deal with this also yourself. I am not supposed to be

Did You Ever Have the Chance to Marry an American Multimillionaire?

your babysitter. This agreement is a comedy. You are a multimillionaire. If you are so rich, why do I still not have a car?"

"I drive you everywhere. You do not need a car. You will always be able to afford a taxi."

Della laughed.

"Really? Oh, yes, especially if I sign the agreement in which you give me nothing. Don't you think that the time can come and you will need my help to drive you somewhere?"

Herbert became mad.

"What are you talking about? We are going to marry and in this moment you tell me that I can be also in a bad situation and would need your help? Shame on you."

"Really? Life is life. Anything can happen. But do not worry. As I told you, I will never marry you."

"Dellishka, you are a different woman now."

"No, my darling, I am the same. You are different. What is going on with you, I do not know. You put a wall between us. I am not coming back to your condo. After being with you for two and a half years, I am in an awful situation. Tomorrow I need to go to college, to go for groceries, to go wherever I need to go. What should I do? Call the multimillionaire Mr. Herbert Samson, and ask him if he is willing to be so kind to drive me, such a poor woman, to buy bread, milk, and tomatoes? Or call for a taxi? Without you I would have a car and would be able to drive well some long time ago. You made me totally depend on you. I trusted you. I was a fool. I am not your possession, Herbert."

"The agreement I gave to you is a normal marriage routine. You made such a big deal from this. Sign the paper and we will arrange the marriage."

"Really? Della doesn't know English very well, does she? If she reads the figures of your wealth, she would jump to the ceiling with joy and sign the papers immediately. This you expected from me, didn't you?"

"No."

"Yes, my dear. Your lawyer made the agreement in the way you requested and paid for. You created a verdict. This paper killed my love and trust in you, it killed our love and our beautiful relationship. Actually, you killed your happiness, you killed yourself."

They finished the dinner.

"Let us take a walk, Dellishka."

"No, thank you. Please, take me home. My home."

They came to her apartment. Della put the agreement on the table and asked Herbert:

"Did you read this ridiculous paper you gave me? Take a look what is written here. Right now."

Herbert turned the pages.

"You know, if I were in your shoes, I would not sign this paper either."

He hugged her.

"You are right. I am sorry. It really doesn't look nice. Tomorrow I will buy you a car."

The next day Herbert took Della to the Buick dealership and bought a gorgeous white Buick Century.

Did You Ever Have the Chance to Marry an American Multimillionaire?

"You see, Herbert, it appeared to be so simple. Thank you. Now I feel more protected with my life in America. You are not going to change your condo, it is obvious. You will stay there. How you wish to continue our relationship is up to you. As I told you many times, I cannot live in your place. To tell you the truth, I no longer have patience for certain things, Herbert. I reached a point in my life where I do not want to waste more time with what displeases me or hurts me. I still love you; I am not going to marry you. I lost the desire, the excitement of our marriage. Unfortunately, you have nothing to offer me as a husband. I am not interested anymore in your endless lunches and trips to Las Vegas. I am not interested in cherishing your fear of flying. Sorry. You can get rid of this fear. But you are simply lazy to do it. I want to see the world and I will."

"Sorry you feel like this. I cannot imagine my life without you."

"I have a driver's license, but I am not ready to drive yet. I need to learn and it is not easy."

"You will drive, Dellishka, do not worry. I will help you."

"Thank you, dear. I will prefer professional lessons. Driving is very serious. Do not forget I am sixty. At sixty years I received my first driver's license. But anyway, thanks for everything. You made my immigration. Actually, you made my America, Herbert, and I will always appreciate this."

After that, Herbert behaved like nothing had happened. It did not matter what Della told him, Herbert continued to talk about marriage, and repeated again and again:

"Before marriage I must separate myself from the children."

He wanted to sell the land that was located somewhere in the county and sell the office building in the city. He had other business obligations that kept him too busy to make his property clear from joint ownership with the children. His mind was tuned only to this. Anger and stubbornness occupied him. He did not want to negotiate with the children.

The more Herbert talked about marriage, the more Della felt she didn't want it. All her being shouted out: "You should not involve yourself in this relationship any longer. He became another person, suspicious and stingy. It is not the Herbert you knew before."

Della joked to herself in the bathroom mirror.

"You told him 'No marriage', but the more you say 'No', the more he says 'Yes'. Really, it would be incredible to be a wife of a multimillionaire. Would you like to try? Take your chance, silly you! This is an unprecedented chance, given once in a lifetime. Just imagine how you would feel by knowing that your spouse was so unbelievably rich. It would be an amazing feeling if you can tell yourself: "My spouse is a multimillionaire!!!" Astonishing sensation!

"It doesn't matter if you have legal rights to his wealth or not. He is your spouse, he loves you. A man in love would do everything for his sweetheart. Especially you know that the figures in this agreement are approximate. He has much more. Arabian horses cost hundreds of thousands. Four jewelry stores (not one, four!!!) cost a fortune. He sold them. He did not sell all the jewelry from the four stores. He keeps it in a huge safe in his garage, so big that it blocks the space for the car. You never asked him to show you the jewelry. Another woman would have. You did not. Why? Silly you. Really, his huge white Lincoln barely fits in the garage and only such an experienced driver like Herbert can park so big a car in such a small space between the safe and the opposite wall. Yes, Della lived in his condo but never asked him what he kept in that safe. There were many moments in their relationship when he was ready to open this secret for her. She was not interested. It was not her business. Della knew that whether she would become his legal wife or not, his property always would be more important to him than she would be. His money was his security, security for a person who deep inside didn't trust himself, and didn't believe that his personality was supposed to be much more important than any money in his account or the treasures in the safe in his garage or in the safe deposit box in the bank.

Did You Ever Have the Chance to Marry an American Multimillionaire?

Herbert told Della many times that he had diamonds and precious stones. Yes, she never asked him to show them to her. Perhaps it was stupid of her. Perhaps, another woman would have behaved differently. But it was Della's own attitude, it was her personality. If he would offer to show them to her, she would look. He definitely was afraid that the showing would be followed by giving, and he was not in the mood for giving. Well, these diamonds and stones did not belong to Della; they were not her business. This was her own way of respecting herself. Yes, we have to respect ourselves.

CHAPTER 38

They did not talk about that stupid agreement. She ignored the subject of marriage, he showed her love and respected her attempts to improve her life in America. Now they became more friends than lovers. They loved to walk in Seaport Village, one of the beautiful places in San Diego.

There were always so many interesting things to see. Unusual paintings, sculptures, handmade articles. Herbert and Della walked around in rapture over the amazingly extraordinary fantasy and creativity of the human mind. Della looked at everything wide-eyed. One picture staggered her: an impenetrable dark wall, in which two hands endeavored to make a hole. There were only two hands in the middle of a big painting, nothing else. These hands told us that they belonged to an intelligent mature woman, who desperately longed for freedom. The hands were well kept, the fingernails covered with red nail polish. The movement of these hands expressed all the passion of the invisible woman who strained her every nerve to tear down that wall of darkness. She had already made a little hole in the wall; you could see behind a quiet expanse of light and peace.

The opening was not big enough to let her through, and her strength was running out. Her hands asked, begged, entreated, yelled, cried "Help!"

Della stopped near that picture. It rooted her to the ground. Della's hands tightened, as she wanted to be together with that woman in her desperate effort to tear through the wall. The nail polish on Della's nails was the same as in the picture and her hands repeated the movements of the painted hands.

At that time, Della struggled hard to put her past out of her mind. Plus, the uncertainty with her situation with Herbert, felt like an adhesive blanket that didn't let her enjoy the moment. She wanted to peel it off, to throw it away, but couldn't.

Some animals change their skin or their fur, which renovates and restores them. She couldn't remove her old skin; she had to deal with her

Did You Ever Have the Chance to Marry an American Multimillionaire?

memories, with the emotional pain of her falling apart relationship, and to make herself comfortable in a new country. Too much. Della was a human being and didn't have the abilities and instincts that God gave to nature's creatures. She was just a woman with all kinds of weaknesses and imperfections who dared to make a tremendous jump—to come to the United States of America at a mature age.

Desperately fighting these feelings that boiled inside her, she walked around, smiling and joking. The painting reflected her emotions. She was aware of being there as if her hands were pictured. She felt herself behind the wall trying to escape from the prison of distress.

Herbert looked at her stunned face; he shouted to his own surprise: "It is you in the picture, your hands are there!"

People around also felt something unusual; they stopped near them and looked at Della. Perhaps her face expressed all the feelings of the invisible woman and she seemed to be the complement of that picture. The emotional impact was so strong that Della felt herself a part of the painting.

A saleswoman appeared in front of them. She took the painting into another room with a special light so they could see the real power of that picture. Della asked the price. They didn't sell the original picture, only copies of it. The price of one copy was $3,000.00. For just two hands.

Astounded by this picture, Della expressed herself in a poem to Herbert:

TO H.

Three years ago I came from Odessa,
Three years were pressed like coffee "Expresso".
It was a high tide,
It was a quick-firing ride.

You came in my life like a great reward,
You helped me so much in this new for me world.
I love you and wish you the best,
I wish you peace, I want you to rest.

Dora Klinova

Remember the picture? I had torn the wall.
I am able to help you, just ask me, just call.
Give, please, the freedom to my soul,
Don't push me to play a different role.

I am telling you: you can fly,
I am certainly sure: you can be in the sky.
You have inside a great power,
Let bloom in you this gorgeous flower.

Yes, you feel the fear, but do it anyway!
You will approach this outstanding day!
You had put yourself in the prison.
I am telling you: there is no reason.

Open your body to the sun and fresh air,
Discard everything what you wear.
You will discover a new wonderful world.
You can do it! The witness is Lord!

Yes, I know you feel the fear.
Please, don't be afraid, my darling, my dear.
You can do it in your life!
And I can be your perfect wife!

Della gave this poem to Herbert. He read it, thanked her, and put it in the safe. He did not show to her any special emotions. Was this poem too naïve in his eyes? Maybe.

CHAPTER 39

LITTLE BY LITTLE Della felt more comfortable to drive. This gorgeous white Buick was the first car Della owned in her entire life. Working for 32 years as an engineer-designer in the Soviet Union, she never was able to afford a car. The feeling that now she could open the door of her own beautiful new car, put herself in the driver's seat, turn the key and drive from her parking lot to any place she needed, made her very proud. Now she could manage college, stores and visiting Rachel. Rachel felt more or less comfortable in the facility. Certainly, she complained, but not so much. Herbert still was willing to pay some money for Rachel.

Della did the very best to establish her life in a new way. She did not want to let herself think about Herbert's oddities in behavior. She did her best to put some colors in their relationship. She tried very hard to be in emotional balance, to be calm with Herbert and to be calm with herself. She could do it in the daytime. At night it was not in her power. As soon she put her head on the pillow hoping to catch a nice sleep, her thoughts danced their own dance. Sigmund Freud said that emotions do not die inside of us. If we suppress them, they eat us from inside. Freud was right. Emotions boiled in Della; it did not matter how hard she tried to calm them down.

A volcano of thoughts demanded to be written down on paper. Overwhelmed with these thoughts, she made herself get up and write out the boiling stuff from her mind. Then she felt a relief, and was able to catch some sleep. Della vigorously wrote at night, amazingly, to her own surprise, in English, not in her native Russian. Beautiful ideas came to her mind during these hours of writing. Della understood that writing became her emotional outlet, an opportunity to bare her innermost thoughts without fear of being criticized or rejected. It was her time to let the ideas flow. She did not worry about spelling; new words came to her, she discovered new phrases, she saw many things in a new light. Her words painted a picture like a brush on a canvas. In English!

She felt a channel in which she gained a liberating understanding of herself and others. It gave her a sense of peace and accomplishment. She had no idea that it was a beginning of her new self realization in American society.

∽∽∽

The spring was gorgeous. Della liked to be near the ocean on the beach. Herbert was not excited to go to the ocean, but because of Della they went sometimes. Della did not like to have her jewelry at the beach and usually left it at home. Once she forgot to do that. She wanted to be in the water so gave her engagement ring to Herbert, who usually waited for her in the shade. He accidentally dropped the ring in the sand. They both frantically tried to find it and couldn't. He became pale.

"It is not a good sign," he whispered. "Dellishka, it is my fault, I will give you another one."

"No, I need this one!" Della said and continued to search. She found it! Herbert jumped with a joy and danced around Della. On the way home Herbert bought gorgeous roses, gave to Della and said:

"God gave the ring back to us. Now we are really engaged. God engaged us."

They came home. Being very happy and exited, Herbert made a picture of the ring with a rose.

Did You Ever Have the Chance to Marry an American Multimillionaire?

A few days later, on Father's Day, Della wrote a poem to Herbert:

To my Herbertchik

The engagement ring was lost on the beach.

It was impossible to find it, to reach.

We thought, we lost it forever.

It is a good saying: "Never say never".

Miraculously the ring was found.

Was it God's message, his sign, his sound?

Very often we think,

We are unable to do many things.

My darling, you can be strong,

You don't need another gong.

Nobody should push you in your life.

Without marriage I AM YOUR WIFE.

I love you.

Happy Father's Day, my love.

Emotional overwhelming pushed Della to write poetry. She never did it before in her native Russian. Now the poems came out from her mind in English. Unknown strong power forced her feverishly to write the lines into her journal.

Herbert showered Della with flowers. And she wrote a poem.

A Flower

Good morning, everybody! Good morning, Sun!
Good morning, Sky! Good morning, Universe!
I am a new flower! I just opened my petals! I am here for you.
Look at me: I am so beautiful; you will never find such wonderful colors.
Each of my petals is a unique picture.
Smell me, breathe me, inhale my aroma in your chest, in your heart.
I am the best in this meadow; you feel my elusive fragrance in the air.
Admire me, enjoy me. Don't postpone any moment of this delight.
You won't see anything like me, for nature never repeats itself.

Did You Ever Have the Chance to Marry an American Multimillionaire?

Take me! I am the best gift! I have the greatest power in the Universe, the power of love.
Give me to your loved one; I will make the vibrations of your love stronger.
Present me to your friend; the friendship will be deeper.
Bring me to your parents. I will illuminate them.
Put me in your girl's hair; I will transform her.
Give me to somebody who is already happy. I will take them to seventh heaven.
You will bathe in their emanation of happiness.
Take me to everyone who grieves; you will feel their appreciation.
If you lose your dearest one, bring me to his grave.
His soul will feel your sign of memory and love.
Give me to those who need support. I will bring them joy.
Do it now, at this moment.
Today I am fresh. I am alive and my spirit is so strong.
Tomorrow will be too late...

Della liked this poem very much and showed it to Herbert. He hugged her and pulled her to his heart.

"You are my gorgeous flower, darling. You wrote this poem about yourself, my Dellishka. Your spirit is so strong."

Herbert continued to invite Della to the solemn ceremonial parties with very rich people. Usually the hostess of the party cordially showed them their seats with their names on the table: "Mr. Herbert Samson and Lady Della Samson." Della looked again and again at the place cards with the name "Lady Della Samson" and thought:

"It sounds great. Enjoy this moment. Who knows when you will have the pleasure to be surrounded with such highly established people again?"

Herbert liked ostentatious things and put the elegant place cards in her purse to keep as a souvenir. Della talked to people, to Herbert, smiled, ate delicious food, danced, and listened to compliments from Herbert and from others. "Am I real?" she silently asked herself. "Who cares? Do not be so serious. Have fun. Why did my dear man put this mask on me? He is not a fool. He is smart. But he is continuing this show with me. Why? It is very simple. He feels comfortable to come to these parties if I am near. Does he use me as a doll? Perhaps. Let him play it. He likes me in this role. Play this puppet role.

Duality in my life? So what? God gives me the opportunity to be here, so enjoy! Who knows, maybe years later I will remember these days as the most exciting time in my life. I will look back and will thank my lucky stars for giving me this experience in life."

Herbert invited Della to Palm Springs. She knew that there was a tramway there. All the way to Palm Springs she tried to convince Herbert to try this experience, to challenge himself. And he did! He was so happy that he overcame his fear of height.

Did You Ever Have the Chance to Marry an American Multimillionaire?

After this ride he became so brave that he ran to a big rock, jumped on it with young vigor, and stood, open to the sky and to the wind, yelling from there to Della:

"Take a picture! A gorgeous picture!"

Herbert looked so young, so handsome, so happy. Della adored him, he looked great. Della made a portrait from this picture and put it on the wall in his bedroom. Near it she hung a picture of an eagle flying above the mountains in the sky. The eagle was hand-painted on a porcelain plate. Herbert had bought it for Della in an Indian resort.

Della hugged him and kissed his eyes: "Herbertchik, the day will come, you will be free from all your fear, and you will fly in the sky like this eagle! And you will wave to me from above with your wing!"

The year 1995 came to the end. Della's birthday approached. It was on the day after Christmas. She always joked: "I let Jesus Christ arrive in the world first. I appeared after." It was her 60th birthday. Herbert made a grandiose party for Della at Tom Ham's Light House restaurant, just above the ocean, on Harbor Drive. All Herbert's children with their families came to be with Della. A lot of people celebrated together with her this special date. How could she make so many friends having lived such a short time in America?

After this Herbert again invited Della for a New Year's Eve at the Hotel Del Coronado. He offered to buy a nice dress for the New Year's party. Della decided to buy the dress herself.

"No, I will do it myself. I want to surprise you, Herbertchik."

She drove to Nordstrom's and bought a gorgeous long white evening dress.

Herbert met her and his eyes shone with admiration.

"You look like my bride, Dellishka!"

"Yes, darling. I am your bride and your beloved forever."

Did You Ever Have the Chance to Marry an American Multimillionaire?

At that New Year's Eve party the "Letterman Show" entertained guests in the Del Coronado Crown Room. Della danced with Herbert near the stage and sang Russian songs to him. One of the Letterman singers came down from the stage and asked Herbert's permission to invite Della to the stage. That singer put Della among the Letterman singers, gave her a microphone, and asked her to sing a Russian song.

And Della did! She sang "Dark Eyes" and danced on the stage. How did it look in the eyes of all these guests, Della did not know and did not care, but she, herself, felt terrific. There was no comparison with her tense feelings three years earlier when Herbert invited her here to the same Crown Room of Del Coronado for her first New Year's Eve in America. Oh, yes, she definitely had become a different person.

Della looked at Herbert. Is he really an American multimillionaire? She talked to herself:

"You are again here, in this most prestigious place in San Diego, with a multimillionaire. Impossible! You came to the United States as a poor refugee from the falling apart Soviet Union and only three months later met an American multimillionaire. How could it happen? Really impossible!

But it did happen, and you were with him all these years having no idea that he is an American multimillionaire."

Really, is this handsome gray-haired man, her lover, her friend, her Herbertchik, a multimillionaire?

He didn't look like a multimillionaire, he didn't dress like a multimillionaire, he didn't eat like a multimillionaire, he didn't act like a multimillionaire. He even did not have a multimillionaire name. Stupid! Stop it! Millionaires are just real people, not saints. They are human beings with all their oddities and problems. They were just smart enough and lucky enough to make money. Now Della understood why Herbert made the prenuptial agreement. He was tremendously rich. It was not about Della. He couldn't marry anybody without a protective agreement.

The waiter brought Champagne.

"Happy New Year, Herbertchik, my dear man, my gift from God! All abundance from the Universe shall come to you!"

CHAPTER 40

A FEW MONTHS later Herbert invited Della for a special event to Long Beach, about a two-hour drive from San Diego. It was a very hot day in Long Beach. They were near the ocean.

"Let us take a quick swim to refresh ourselves. I took our bathing stuff, yours is here," Della said.

"You go, Dellishka, I will wait for you in the shade."

"Better go into the water, it is hot even in the shade."

"No, I am okay here."

He did not want to change and was sitting in his long trousers. She ran into the water and jumped immediately out.

"Let us go back to the car with air-conditioning." She put the air-conditioner on high. Suddenly Herbert's eyes started to rotate in different directions. This scared Della to death.

"Herbert, what is going on?"

"I do not know. I am out of my mind. My head doesn't belong to me!"

"I will call emergency!"

"No! I had it before. It will go away, just let me rest and breathe deeply."

"Did you ask the doctor?"

"Yes, I did. He doesn't know what it is unless he can see it."

"Please, let me call emergency."

"No, Della. Our show will start soon. We will enjoy the show. If you call emergency, they will keep me in the hospital who knows how long. They want money from my insurance. I do not care. I am okay already."

"We are not far away from the theater. Let me drive."

"No, no, I am fine."

His eyes became normal. They arrived at the theater. He excused himself and went to the restroom. Della called to Herbert's son Clint in San Diego and told him what happened.

"What should I do, Clint?"

"Do not be in the sun. Today is a hot day. Come home. We will see how he feels tomorrow."

"He needs to drive all the way. I do not drive on freeways yet."

"He is a good driver. He will be fine."

Everything looked okay. Herbert ate the dinner, they watched a nice show. He joked and said he felt great. They drove back home late.

"You panicked for nothing. Stop worrying about me. I am solid as a rock," Herbert told Della.

"Herbert, yes, I am worrying. Something strange is going on with you. Rent out your condo to somebody and move out to another house. Take yourself out from these bad vibrations in your house. If you change the house, I will come back to you. I will live with you."

"Come on, Della, stop it! Moving is a disaster. I do not want it. I am perfectly fine in my condo."

"Sorry, Herbert, I do not believe it. But you are your own boss; it is your choice."

Actually Herbert looked okay, but more often he felt deadly tired. Della also felt tired. She couldn't understand what was going on with her emotionally. She became too nervous near Herbert.

She understood that she should thank God that a man like Herbert was with her even though she said "No" to their marriage. She criticized herself: "Stop being so demanding. Nothing is perfect in life. Something good always goes with something negative. Nobody is perfect, and he is wonderful. He is great. He cannot marry anybody without protecting his wealth. Did his agreement insult you? Yes. So what? He was mad at you. But after this he bought you a gorgeous car. By the grace of God your life in the United States is protected. Be grateful!"

No matter what she told herself, it didn't help. She felt strong inner resistance to be with Herbert. Della tried hard to ignore it, but she couldn't. Meanwhile, she was sinking into the vortex of new life in America that swallowed her days, weeks and months.

Did You Ever Have the Chance to Marry an American Multimillionaire?

She did not bother him or Clint with questions. Being near Herbert and his family for all these years she established a rule for herself: Never ask questions. Whatever they wanted to share with her she appreciated. The rest was not her business.

She knew that the relationship with Herbert was slowly falling apart, and felt lonesome even when he was near. She did not feel connection with him anymore; he was deep inside with his own thoughts and problems. With Della he played a role of a happy man, but now it was just a role, and Della knew this.

Della did not want to look anymore at that premarital agreement. What evil power pushed her darling man to create this disgusting monster?

She put the agreement far away from her eyes on the very top shelf of her closet. She decided to keep this document, being sure that many years later it will become a great souvenir of her American life.

Della understood that she was a challenge for Herbert. She came to America with a great dream to start a new life. Herbert's dream was to find a woman to finish his life with. They had quite opposite goals in life: start and finish. They had different desires: to fling the door wide open to the entire Universe or pull down the blinds of the windows in his condo. To breathe deeply with the whole breast and expose the face to all the fresh winds in the world or to pull the hat down over the eyes and ears. To fly or to crawl, to feel the fresh wind of freedom or to lock themselves in the prison of the mirrored living room in Herbert's condo where he was going to spend the rest of his life.

With Della Herbert could do the greatest things, be healthy and feel young. She could open for him a new world. She was able to bring into his soul all the stars from the sky. With his money and with her energy, with her ability to find and to create the greatest enjoyment, he could drink out all thirst for life. With these combined efforts they could be the happiest couple in the world.

Della became the greatest test of his strength. He was still vigorous enough to pass this life exam, he could manage this. But he got too frightened. His fear took away his fortitude. He let this conflict grow in his soul. He couldn't climb this peak. This mountain was beyond Herbert's power to conquer.

CHAPTER 41

WE RUSH, OUR lives run away, week by week, month by month, who knows where? The year 1996 slowly but firmly dissolved into oblivion. Herbert invited Della for a New Year's Party at the Hotel Marriott in Seaport Village. Joyful, festive, merry atmosphere, happy, cheerful faces around. Herbert did not want to miss any dance, he again and again pulled Della from her chair and ran with her to the dance circle. He hugged her, kissed her. They joked and danced, they laughed and danced, they chatted cheerfully and danced.

"Herbertchik, you are outstanding tonight!"

"I am with you, my darling Dellishka!"

The entire world told Della: this is your moment of life, this evening is a gift from God, enjoy it! Della repeated to herself a thousand times:

"Enjoy! Enjoy! Enjoy! It is your paradise! You are in heaven!" But her mind continuously whispered to her: *It is your Goodbye party with Herbert.* The New 1997 Year arrived. They silently drank their Champagne, looking in each other eyes, then suddenly they both jumped up from their chairs, squeezed each other in an embrace that made the two of them one essence, one soul, one body. They continued to stay being afraid to release their arms.

They both felt that it was their farewell New Year's Eve. Oh, they did not want it. NO! NO! NO! She whispered in his ear:

"I will not let you go, I love you so much, Herbertchik, you will be strong, young, healthy. I will make you a King of the Universe, my King! Make only one serious movement, find another house to live in and I will immediately move with you. I do not need any marriage, I want just to be near you. Get out from your condo, please."

Della should not have said anything about the condo. Reminding Herbert about the condo immediately changed his mood. He knew that this condo might kill him, but to get out from it was unbearable for him. Invisible vibrations glued him to it.

Did You Ever Have the Chance to Marry an American Multimillionaire?

After the party was over, they went to Della's apartment. Herbert wanted passionately to make love, but was unable to do it, and he became upset.

"Do not worry, Herbertchik, you are too tired, you will be vigorous in the morning!"

"I just want to let you know, my darling woman, no one man in your entire life loved you as much as I do. You are my Queen and always will be. I am telling this from the depth of my heart. You are a bright shiny sun for me, and I am just a little dull candle near you." He repeated this again and again.

Life continued in its routine way. Herbert was near Della, but so far away in his mind. She had tried different approaches with him to make him closer; it did not work. Della often felt so unpleasant and uncomfortable being around him that many times she excused herself, declining his invitations for a lunch or a dinner. She also sent him home when he wanted to stay with her the night. Tolerating him had become increasingly difficult. She felt that she was falling into depression.

"NO! NO! No depression, please, God, save me from this!"

Herbert looked very tired. They had dinner at Della's place, eating borsch and stuffed peppers that she prepared for him and he loved so much. After dinner he put many bottles of supplements and vitamins on the table and took a bunch of pills after they finished eating. Della looked at the bottles. Many vitamins were repeated in the supplements.

"You overdose yourself with these vitamins. Who told you to take so many of them?"

"Nobody. I chose them myself."

"Please, go to the doctor, you work too much, you need good nutritious food, fresh squeezed juices, not from the cans. At least two glasses daily. Ask your housekeeper to do it for you. Or let me do it. May I do it for you right now? I have carrots, apples, celery, ginger, the perfect combination for a healthy drink."

"No, no, I hate carrot juice. Thank you."

Again she asked him to take a vacation.

"Our relationship is falling apart. It depresses me, it depresses you. Let us take a train to go somewhere, or a cruise. On a cruise you are visiting different cities and the hotel, I mean the ship, goes with you. It will heal our relationship. We can go to Alaska, to Mexico, even to Hawaii."

"Oh, my wife and I went on an Alaskan cruise. Incredible. It was the only cruise I took in my life. I will never forget it."

"So, if you like it, let us take a cruise again."

"No, it was very expensive. My wife paid about five thousand dollars."

"For Alaska? What are you talking about? A seven-day cruise costs about $850 to $950 per a person. I saw an advertisement."

"It depends. Maybe it was an expensive ship plus the best cabin with the balcony. She decided that once in a lifetime it was worth to pay good money for the best trip."

"She was right. You deserve the best all the time, not once in a lifetime. Does it cost money? Yes. That is why you make money—to enjoy life and yourself. We can even take a cruise to Hawaii."

"No, not now. I cannot leave the center for so many days. It needs my care."

"The center needs your care? How about yourself, Herbert? You need care! If the cruise is expensive for you, let us go by train somewhere. Anywhere!"

"I am fine, do not worry about me."

"Okay, you cannot leave the center. Why don't we go to the SPA, to get some professional massages, to nourish our bodies in the sauna, in the steam room? I am trying to eat healthy, but good advice from a good nutritionist would be great. We are not young, we must support our bodies. I have an advertisement about a special workshop how physical and spiritual health coincides. Look at this. They focus on the importance of nourishing our mind, body, and soul through physical exercise, nutrition, and the word of God. They even bring a quote from the Bible:

As 1 Corinthians 6:19-20 says, *"Do you not realize that your body is the temple of the Holy Spirit who lives in you and was given to you by God? You do not belong to yourself, for God bought you with a high price. So you must honor God with your body."*

"Dellishka, dear, they want to make money, using Bible quotes for this. People make their business. We do not need to be involved in this. I am perfectly fine."

"Well, Herbert, I am not so strong as you. I am not fine, I need a break."

"Let us go to Las Vegas for three days."

"Aren't you tired of Las Vegas, Herbert? We go there every 2 to 3 months."

"Tired of Las Vegas? Never. Always something new there."

"No thank you, Herbert. I am fed up with Las Vegas. There are so many other gorgeous places to visit."

CHAPTER 42

Della's interlocutor was her own image in the bathroom mirror. She looked into her own eyes asking herself:

"Why do you behave with him like a beggar? You do want to help him, don't you? He doesn't want your help! Do you feel obligated to him? Why? Because you love him? Or because you do not want to lose him? Perhaps both. If he gave you this crazy agreement, why do you feel any obligations? A cruise is too expensive for him? He becomes stingy. Massages and Spa are also too expensive for him. Let him keep his money, let him take his endless care for his center and make more money. You do not need to be involved in this craziness. You go somewhere and give yourself some joy. Enough is enough."

A protest arose in her. She decided to go to Hawaii. Yes, Hawaii! Her Russian friend, an owner of a Russian tourist company, offered her an affordable trip to Hawaii. She immediately paid for the trip. Herbert was very disappointed with Della's new adventure; he did not expect that Della would dare to go by herself to Hawaii.

"I will not go by myself. I am going with a group of Russian people. Some of them I know pretty well. I do not want to discuss this subject anymore with you. You continue to sit in your center. It is your choice. I will enjoy Hawaii. Period."

She flew to Honolulu. During the long flight Herbert was in her mind constantly.

"He did for me so many incredible things, he told me so many wonderful words, he encouraged me so much as a woman. In his eyes I was the most beautiful and clever lady. He repeated that I was sent to him as a divine gift to open his soul and to explore all deep warm feelings that he was not able to realize and to release during his entire life. Who knows why he behaves now this way, but thanks for everything he gave to me. My low bow to you, dear God, for Herbert. Please, help me and help him, please, please, dear God..."

Did You Ever Have the Chance to Marry an American Multimillionaire?

Hawaii offered its invisible smell of happiness. Heaven. Being in this paradise, Della felt so sad. She knew she was losing Herbert. It was so painful.

The next day she came to the beach with her Russian friend, the leader of their group. He had been many times in Hawaii, so he knew a good beach to swim. He left Della in the shallow water and swam away farther into the ocean. Warm water, blue endless sky. Della grew up near the warm Black Sea in sunny Odessa, but never experienced such a gorgeous place as this.

"Enjoy, feel the fullness of life, breathe deeply, be happy as a bird. God is with you."

She repeated these words like a spell. She did, but couldn't get rid of sad thoughts about Herbert. He chased her here, thousands of miles away. Della was haunted by thoughts; they did not help her to solve her problems. They just kept running in a circle taking away her energy and strength. She went into the water, literally trying to wash this delusion off herself. Herbert strongly invisibly attacked her. Della became angry at herself.

"What is going on with you, dear? Herbert is not like he was before. So what? Is it a disaster? Are you homeless? Hungry? Are you going to die tomorrow? You don't have money to buy bread? What is the tragedy? Look around… You are in America, moreover, you are in Hawaii. He will never come here. He is a multimillionaire, you are a poor refugee from the USSR. You are here, he is not. It is his problem, not yours. He put himself in a prison. Is he getting old? He is only 75. So, you escaped from his prison. Enjoy the freedom!!!"

She looked around. Her friend swam somewhere far away. Nobody was near. Only the wide ocean was around, the deep blue sky above, and beautiful Honolulu in front of her. Freedom! Freedom! Freedom!!!!

Della jumped in the water singing, yelling, laughing, making a big noise and suddenly her tongue shouted out loudly vulgar Russian slang words she had never used before. She sang these dirty Russian words, roaring to herself. Perhaps, Honolulu never heard such a loud vulgar song in Russian language:

"F..ck you, I am in Hawaii! F..ck you, I am in Hawaii! La la la, F..ck you!!!"

A Japanese man swam up closer to her.

"You are singing a beautiful song. What is the language?"

"Russian."

"What is the song about?"

"How great Hawaii is!"

"You look so happy! May I sing it with you?"

"Of course, repeat after me the words!"

They took their hands, jumped together in the water singing loudly these dirty Russian words. Different people came over joining their circle. The expanded ensemble danced and loudly sang, repeating this Russian nasty slang with different accents. Della laughed, thinking that if the police appeared here, she wouldn't be arrested, because police won't understand these terrible Russian words either. More people wanted to have a good time: the circle became huge.

Suddenly in the middle of the circle from the bottom of the ocean, like a Neptune, a man appeared and in clear Russian language loudly took up the "song".

"F...ck you! We are in Hawaii!!!" It was Della's friend, the leader of the tourist Russian group. With great pleasure he also expressed himself with these dirty words in the middle of the warm Pacific Ocean. Only the two of them understood the comedy of this situation and laughed themselves to tears. Della was sure that never before did Honolulu hear such an enthusiastic chorus with such strong releasing words. Dirty words help! My God, it became great psychotherapy for Della, a relief from sinking feelings, a comforting release.

Della jumped, played with the water, made a halo of splashes around herself that sparkled with all colors of the rainbow under the Hawaiian sun. She sparkled herself. She danced, yelling up to the sky:

"My precious man, my dear Herbert, you brought so much happiness into my life, so much brightness, so much love, and so much pain. F...ck this pain, I want only love, love, and love! I love you!!!! Do you hear me in

Did You Ever Have the Chance to Marry an American Multimillionaire?

California? You are sitting there all your life and do not allow yourself to see the beauty of the world. I am in Hawaii, and you, an American multimillionaire, are not. It is your choice, but not mine. I will see the entire world. I escaped from the Soviet Union Iron Curtain, I will not let you hold me in your prison. No way, darling! I appreciate everything what you did for me. I am so grateful! I love you so-o-o-o much! Be well!! I am sending to you all abundance from the Universe! I am the child of the Universe! This Universe belongs to me!"

Della imagined unzipping her head, unzipping the skin of her entire body and let out all the pain, all the demons escape from her mind. Out! Out! Out! Sink in the ocean!!!

"I am free, I am free, fre-e-e-e!!! Ufff!!!"

It was a great experience in psychotherapy, a relief from depression. It became an incredible cure for her mind. Della freed herself.

CHAPTER 43

Herbert met her in the airport.

"How is Hawaii?" His voice was full of grief.

"You do not know what you are missing. You carry this stupid fear of flying all your life. You can cure yourself from that in a few months just taking a few sessions with a psychotherapist. But you don't want to. You are too lazy to improve yourself. You are your own enemy. Plus, you kept your wife from seeing the world. Why did she obey you?"

"Because she loved me."

"Yes, she did, so do I. You used her love for your own comfort and laziness. Yes, laziness. You had a flight accident many years ago. So what? People have car accidents on the road, but they continue to drive anyway. I've learned that it's not what happens to people. It's what they do about it.

"I will fly all around the world. I will not cherish your cowardice. No way, my darling!"

Della decided to tell him everything what she thought about their situation.

"Your wife had three children and business. She was older and did not have energy to fight with your idiotic attitude about flying. Her mind was too busy. And you used it. It was a crime against yourself and against her.

"I am curious: for whom do you collect all your fucking money? For yourself? For your children? Or for the bank? The bank is very comfortable to handle and use your money. They do, you do not! You just feel great satisfaction feeling the possession of these millions. You do not let yourself take a cruise because it is expensive. Shame on you! Or because your center needs your attention. Nonsense. Your money needs your attention, not the center. Money has become your shackles. You will not be able to spend all your money in a few lifetimes.

Did You Ever Have the Chance to Marry an American Multimillionaire?

"You cannot allow yourself to take off a couple of weeks to rejuvenate yourself. It is still not enough money for you. Go ahead, big multimillionaire, make more money. Live in your dark stinking condo, I am not with you."

"I missed you so much, and you are talking to me in this way?"

"Sorry to tell you this, but nobody else will tell you the truth, only me. This trip to Hawaii was not a joy for me without you. It was painful. It was a fight with depression. You were 24/7 on my mind. I couldn't stop thinking about you for a moment. You are chasing me. I love you too much. I am not able to run away from you. You broke my heart into pieces."

After Hawaii Della promised herself to do everything possible to improve her health, to make fresh squeezed juices, to gain strength, to widen her spirituality, and not to let Herbert stress her. She talked to Herbert mentally:

"You have money, Herbert? This was what you told me immediately, during the first hour when you met me. Are you a multimillionaire? Good. You do not enjoy life. I will. I will be a billionaire of joy. I will celebrate life, I will cherish each day of my existence!"

Herbert continued to come, and Della continued to prepare good Russian dinners for him. Sometimes they went to the movies or to a concert. Sometimes they went together to visit Rachel.

May 3, 1997 was special for Herbert, his 75th birthday. Della had asked him to make a party, to invite all his children. He did not want to. His relationship with his children was very tense. So Della and Herbert were sitting in a nice restaurant above the ocean, just the two of them.

"Look at this beauty, Herbert. Look at the sunset. God painted the sky, it is so gorgeous. We have everything to be happy like these birds above us, but we are not. At least, I am very sad. We lost something very valuable in our relationship. I do not know how to deal with this. It is very painful for me. I cannot change anything, but I know that each of your visits takes a lot of my energy and I feel exhausted afterward. I am not interested anymore in these useless lunches, dinners and empty conversations. We are running nowhere, my darling. I am very sorry."

"I miss you, Dellishka."

"Try to understand my point of view. We are in different boats now, my darling. Unfortunately. You are a well established man, and I, after being so many years with you, must somehow establish myself in America. I feel like I am again starting my immigration. I do not want to be in pain anymore."

"I will not give you pain, I promise. Please, forgive me this prenuptial agreement. I looked at it again. If it would be given to me, I would never sign it. You are right. I will do everything to make you happy."

"No, Herbertchik, you will not. The Bible says: "I am who I am." So are you. You are who you are. You have a tremendous amount of money, and I am on government support, actually on welfare. Your money will be always between us. The biggest bank account can't replace the power of love. I am with you so many years, and all these years you kept me on this

Did You Ever Have the Chance to Marry an American Multimillionaire?

welfare. Our relationship is actually over, and now you let me go without offering me a penny."

"I will support you."

Della shook her head, laughing: "Will you? We will see. Let me go, Herbert."

"The Jewish High Holidays are approaching. I would love to go with you to synagogue services," Herbert said.

"This I will do with my pleasure, Herbert. I will get tickets for you. Remember, Rachel and I are members of Temple Emmanuel. They are supposed to send us tickets. I will give you Rachel's tickets; you will not need to pay money. Now take me home, Herbert, please."

He brought Della home. She kissed him on the cheek and got out of the car.

"Let us take a break, Herbertchik. I need my peace. Let us see how we will feel about each other if we meet not so often. As soon as I get tickets for the High Holidays at the temple, I will let you know."

CHAPTER 44

No, Herbert did not want to be without Della. Two days later he invited her to Hotel Del Coronado. He talked again about the agreement and how it was extremely important to sign it. Della became exhausted after this dinner and asked him to give her a break and try not to call her. But a few days later he called and talked to her an hour and a half on the phone.

That night, like many other nights, Della's sleep was restless, and her mind was filled with thoughts of Herbert. Finally, unable to sleep, she got out of bed and let the words spill out onto paper, hoping to get some relief.

A Poetical Response to after-birthday

dinner in Hotel Del Coronado and to an hour and a half telephone conversation a few days later

My dear Dellishka, what is the matter?
Sign, please, the paper, I will feel much better,
I cannot love you without the paper,
Agreement will make me much safer.

I promise to give you some donation.
I am a gentleman, if you be a nice girl,
If you deserve my better score,
Then I will make donation a bit more.

When you will be one hundred years old,
You will have million dollars and gold.
I am puzzled, why you don't want my donation?
More than two years we repeat this conversation.

Did You Ever Have the Chance to Marry an American Multimillionaire?

I am a gentleman; I love you so much,
My love is eternal, your heart should be touched.
I bought you a diamond bracelet on Valentine Day,
I didn't hear any thanks, one "Thank you" you didn't say.

I am entitled to own all money,
I don't care how will feel my wife, my dear honey.
I don't see from you any appreciation.
You didn't make on my birthday any presentation.

You are not innocent anymore,
You are not that person you had been before.
You think only about my dollars,
This made me worry, I lost the goal of life, all its colors.

You will be a citizen pretty soon,
You will jump from me to the moon.
You will run away to Russia with all my money.
How can I find you in Russia, my dear honey?

Specially you have now a car,
(Oh, such a terrible mistake, my heart has a big scar.)
Why are you so persistent to drive?
I can give always a ride to my darling wife.

You made between us a tense situation
Sending to college the application.
I cannot handle this situation.
I hate your Yoga and meditations.

I have to stop with you my communication!
If I am afraid to fly,
You are also supposed to hate the sky.
That is what I am paying you for!

Dora Klinova

Donna named you "Russian gold digger",
And I agree, your fault is much bigger.
She said, "Be careful, Della is smart,
Don't open to her any of your cards.

She will grab all your money and live her life,
And you will have a mirage, not a wife."
Donna is 100% right,
I couldn't sleep a whole night.

You pushed me to pay for Jennifer's education.
This brought me additional aggravation.
It was not your business!
Please, pay me the compensation!

I won't give to you a penny!
Do you think I am a "Bank of America"?
All this stuff just makes me hysterical.

Why in this case I should stop to eat your food?
You cook delicious, your dinners are so good!
I am a gentleman, you invited me, I ate, so what?
But I won't give you anymore my support!

You are so terrific in bed,
Oh, my God, with you I can everything forget.
I love you with all my heart,
But you are refusing to sleep with me; it hurts.

I spoiled you, I did everything what you want,
I gave you a lot. I gave you too much,
You took advantage of me.
Now I want to eat your food and sleep with you for "free".

Did You Ever Have the Chance to Marry an American Multimillionaire?

I am a gentleman, I really enjoy your organic food,
Your body is so nice and your soups are so good!
Why should I give you presents? Love is free.
You must pay to me back your fee.

I am a businessman, you are for me such a great deal,
Especially with your homemade meal.
American women don't like to cook.
I gave you promises and hung you up on my "hook".

Sign the paper, it will help me to put you on "Hold",
And to keep my money and gold.
Dellishka and money, everything will be mine!
Oh, I have the greatest Jewish mind!

I am a genius, I am a King,
You have to believe me, I gave you an engagement ring.

What is the matter? This lady from farshtinkener Russia
Made from my great plan a mess, a terrible kasha.
You made me mad! You made me sad!
"Every sheet in this paper is a piece of sh...", you said,
And tore the paper directly into my hat!

I calculated every dollar and sum
Which I gave to you and to my two sons.
My sons are millionaires, they will be fine,
You have nothing, you should be mine.

I am a gentleman, I always keep my word.
I will open for you a new world.
We will make cruises to Mexico and Canada,
Our next will be to Europe, and then to Grenada.

Dora Klinova

As I promised, I bought for myself a new Cadillac.
With your kind permission
I can always give you a ride
To the Welfare Office and Housing Commission.

I showered you with so many temptations,
What for you continued your education?
I gave you lunches, dinners, shows; just eat and look.
Instead, you keep reading these hated books.

You write for me poems, what I need them for?
They make just garbage in my drawer,
I am tired to read them and to count,
Plus, I cannot deposit them to my Bank account.

This is another one, it is so long,
Really, look at this length, look!
It is not a poem, it is almost a book!

I try to forget you, I read them and throw away...
But my mind brings you again and again in my way!

I did for you so many good things,
To Welfare Office almost at night I could you bring.
You lived with me, you had been mine,
I took my time to stay with you in welfare's line.

I showed to all your friends that you are my queen,
Once to welfare I drove you in my limousine.
It made you sad, you became mad.
Let us better sit together near TV and take a nap.
A nap is so exciting! Why do you need your boring writing?

Did You Ever Have the Chance to Marry an American Multimillionaire?

You don't need a man,
You do everything yourself, you can!
Now you take computers and acting class!
Laila, quick give me water in glass.

There are plenty of women, I will find a wife,
With her I will accomplish my life,
But they are all "brr, fuuu…" to compare to Dellishka.
They will only cause diarrhea in my kishkes.

Stop, immediately stop! I don't understand,
Why I created this rubbish in my head?
Do I need a stupid wife?
I will be bored with her for the rest of my life.

My God, I do something completely wrong.
I lost all the beauty of my heart's song.
These thoughts make me depressed.
I cannot relax, I cannot rest.

Della doesn't love me anymore.
Why is she supposed to, what for?
Did I bring in her soul peace and comfort?
I stopped to give her all my support.

Maybe I should say a thousand times "Sorry"
For causing my dearest Della so much worry.
Maybe, I should ask forgiveness and bow low to her,
My adorable Russian lady with gorgeous red hair…

P.S.
How do you think, Herbertchik, is it enough here?
Why all this nonsense did I have to hear?

It is an eternal fight between love and money.
Alas, money is your sweetest honey…
Yes, love is a treasure, love is great,
But maybe for love is too late?

I made you worry.
I am NOT sorry!

Dellishka

Della mailed this long poem to Herbert. No reaction. For a few weeks they did not see each other. One day Della came to the bank. While Della parked her car, a big splendid Lincoln appeared in the parking spot next to her. It was Herbert. What power brought him at that particular moment to the bank? What power pushed him to park next to her? There were plenty of other parking spots around.

He parked faster than she was able to do, bounced out from his car, and ran to the bank's entrance. He didn't see Della.

She signaled. He turned round, noticed her, and raced over to her car. She opened the car's window. His eyes lit up.

"Oh, my God! You? I cannot believe my eyes. How are you?"

What do American people usually answer to this question? It doesn't matter how they feel, the answer always is:

"I am fine."

"Come out from the car, please. I am so glad to see you."

He stood near Della, gaunt, but well dressed, in a new suit and tie. Della asked him:

Did You Ever Have the Chance to Marry an American Multimillionaire?

"Do you miss me?"

"Very much."

"Do you think about me?"

"All the time."

"I feel it. You think about me and your thoughts put you in my mind. I cannot understand how it works; it is a connection on another level. I know exactly the time when you think about me. I am tired of you, Herbert. Leave me alone, please. What do you want from me?"

"Nothing. You will never sign the paper."

"Again you talk about this agreement. It shields your eyes from me. You don't see me anymore. Now this crazy paper is more important for you than me."

"Of course, it is important. I am an American. And I am a businessman. You don't understand American laws."

"It is a great idea to discuss this question in a parking lot, isn't it? Stop it, please. Tell me better, did you find a woman already?"

"Oh, yes, I have two of them. They are both Americans. No more Russians for me."

"Poor man, this Russian lady made you so exhausted. I feel so sorry that you had such a terrible time with me. Della was such an awful experience in your life."

His face changed. He looked in Della's eyes seriously.

"Each night I thank God for you, Dellishka. I will never forget you, never ever. Just remember this all your life. You will be always in my heart. I look forward to spending the Jewish High Holidays with you."

"When I have tickets, I will call you. Yes, I know you keep me in your heart even though I am not with you anymore. I cannot take it. Disconnect from me. Please. Find a woman for yourself and let me go. If you have two, you have none, do you know this?"

"I need time to choose. One is very nice, but she is a Catholic. By the way, she is younger than you! Another is a Jewish lady, good also, but she is too involved with her children and grandchildren. I need to choose. I am working on this now."

"How do you share yourself between their beds?"

"No, I don't sleep with them yet."

"Where did you find them?"

"At a singles party."

"Oh, congratulations. Now you are running around to single parties. I didn't know that American millionaires hang out at singles parties. Why did you catch only two women? Usually at singles parties there are twenty women for one man. You should be more energetic to find more. Be careful, there is a lot of aids around. Good luck!"

Della hugged him and left. This conversation twirled in her mind. What is wrong with Herbert? He is smart and he can keep secrets. Nobody knew his business. And now he talked as a boy who needed to boast with his successes between girls. No, it is not like him. He lost his confidence in himself; he became fussy.

She became angry with herself.

"Stop thinking about him. You cannot teach an old dog new tricks. Immediately stop it. You must do your own life. Let him go!"

CHAPTER 45

DELLA RECEIVED TICKETS for the High Holidays and called Herbert. He was so glad to talk to her.

"Thank you, darling. I am dreaming and waiting for the cherished time to spend the Holidays with you."

She gave him the tickets for both holidays. They went to Rosh Hashanah together, sitting all the long service holding hands. They really missed each other very much.

A couple of weeks later Herbert invited Della for dinner. When he brought her home, before she left the car, he gave her back the ticket for Yom Kippur.

He explained:

"I got an invitation for Yom Kippur and for 'break of the fast.' I would like to take this invitation."

"Without me?"

"I was asked to come myself. I know the ticket cost money. Here is $100.

"Take away your money." She angrily threw the $100 back at him.

"I do not mean to make you upset." He took the money and put it back carefully in his wallet.

"Do I know these people?"

"Yes. I do not feel so good to visit them without you, I know, it is not nice, but they want to talk to me personally. Honestly, Dellishka, I am all mixed up with our situation. Maybe it is a good idea to go to them myself."

"Go, have fun! Goodbye!"

Who invited him without Della? Della's dearest best friends. She knew them from Odessa. They arrived in San Diego a year after Della. At that time her relationship with Herbert was blossomed. When Della introduced them to Herbert, one of the first questions they asked Della:

"Do you know all his sizes?"

"Yes, I do," she answered laughing. "Is this a new Odessa's way to ask about intimacy?"

They were very close during all the years of Della's relationship with Herbert, and certainly they knew in detail what was going on between Della and Herbert. Della trusted them and shared with them her pain.

Della came home and talked to herself in the mirror.

"Well, a good lesson for me. How many years do you know these 'friends'? Many years, since your childhood. How many good things you did for them when they arrived to America from Odessa? Let them count. You were able to help them and you did, good for you; you were powerful near Herbert, a rich American. They clung to you, using you as much as they could. Without Herbert you lost your power and became for them as a shot-out used cartridge that belonged only to garbage. Good! They will cling to Herbert now.

"Learn to recognize the line when your best friends start taking advantage of you using your love for them. Yes, it is a lesson. Gain your wisdom, my dear. Shit happens. Learn to be wiser."

As Della was told later, to please Herbert these so-called "friends" started actively searching for a woman to put her in lonesome Herbert's bed. They found another Russian woman and decided to introduce her to Herbert. When? During the Jewish High Holiday, knowing that Della was going to spend these holidays with Herbert. For this action they chose Yom Kippur, the day of forgiveness, no less. They invited them behind Della's back. How to name it? Betrayal? Treachery? Meanness? Jealousy or envy? All together.

There is a Russian saying: "There are always green flies that fly around the fat piece of meat." A rich American with a lot of money was definitely a fat portion for these "green flies."

Did You Ever Have the Chance to Marry an American Multimillionaire?

How did Della feel about their behavior? It was, of course, awfully painful. But somehow she was not surprised. Being with Herbert, she felt a cloud of others jealousy and envy all the time.

Maybe this was the point why Della often did not feel happy. Jealousy can poison every great event in our life, destroy happiness, sparkling eyes become dull, joy disappears when jealousy emits its vibrations at us.

We feel emptiness inside and a heavy stone in our heart. We should learn to recognize jealous people. These negative vibrations usually come from the closest people, friends and even relatives. Why? Because only they know more than anybody else how you are happy. Alas, not everybody enjoys when you are happy.

Jealousy has its own face. Your recent best friends being overwhelmed with envy look at you with cold eyes, and each of their words pinch and belittle you. We should find strengths to turn them out from our house and from our life immediately.

We never know what is going on in the souls of other people, even if they are our dearest friends or relatives.

Once in a conversation Della mentioned that emigration changes people and we have to accept this. The person she was talking to disagreed with her:

"No, emigration doesn't change people, it opens their real faces, it shows who is who, it takes the masks off from them. If they have a good heart, they would remain the same; if they have a junk soul, you would see it here."

Perhaps God wants us to meet a few wrong people before meeting the right ones. When we finally meet the right person, we will know how to be grateful for that gift.

Della learned the wisdom: "Be proud of yourself if somebody is envious of you. Envious people are weak, they let junk to be in their souls, they need to grow, they need to put God in their souls. Bless them, forgive them, and continue to be happy."

We are surrounded by people. Some of them are given to us: family, classmates, coworkers; some we choose ourselves. People are not perfect; we need to learn to live with them. Meeting new people, each of us goes through his own way to recognize potential friends or those whom are better to forget for the rest of our life. Are we always able to do this?

It is said in Russia: "To recognize a friend you need to eat a full big bag of salt together with him."

Life is our best teacher. Della went through extremely harmful situations. It was her learning process. Della is sure it had been her fate to go through terrible circumstances in life to become the person she is now. These painful life lessons pushed her to change her attitude completely and not to be a sheep anymore.

Della learned: life itself puts everything in its place over the years. We became wiser and smarter. Life became easier to live; we see and gain more joy. People start to respect us and the miserable ones disappear.

They don't dare to touch us; they somehow understand that we are already not in the field for their miserable activities. New people try to reach us. We start to respect ourselves. It comes easily. Our personality grows up, we find ourselves on a higher level of consciousness. From this position we are able to forgive all of those who put us in tremendous pain in the past; we look at them with different eyes, we understand that they are who they are and unable to behave better. So, let them go. Looking at them from our new higher life position, we can easily leave them behind.

As Della was told later, Herbert immediately offered the Russian woman he was introduced to, to move into his condo. It was Ales. What a success! Della's "friends" advised Ales to accept his offer immediately, without any thinking, without any hesitation. She followed their advice, grabbed

Did You Ever Have the Chance to Marry an American Multimillionaire?

the opportunity, left her job, gave away her apartment and furniture and moved in with Herbert.

Well, perhaps for Ales Herbert appeared as a Firebird, but why did Herbert rush to put a barely known woman in his home and in his bed? What was the cause of such a rush?

CHAPTER 46

When do we plead to God? Usually when we cannot help ourselves and everything is going wrong in our life. Then we are crying for support.

"God, dear God, I know, there was a reason that Herbert came into my life. Did You, dear God, put us together to solve some issues we carry from our past lives? Will we meet each other again in our next lifetime? I couldn't continue to live this way with Herbert. I am not so strong, my darling God. Give me the power, please... I know we still love each other. It doesn't matter that he is with another woman. Give me the strength, please, tell me what I am supposed to do now. I go to the Reform Synagogue to be closer to You. They pray in Hebrew there and I do not understand the prayers. Let me be closer to you, please..."

Della found another temple. Was this an answer to her prayers? She didn't know. Somewhere in 1985, back to Odessa, Della became very sick, almost near death. No doctor could help her. She wasn't able to work. Her inner voice yelled:

Do you want to die? If so, go ahead! Do it! Die! Right now! To die? No way!!! Life is too good!!! Forget about doctors. Your life is in your own hands. Search! Find another source to be healthy. Recognize it! Use it!

Search... It was easy to say. Where to search? How? In what direction should she go if she didn't have strengths at all and the doctors issued her a disabled certificate?

"You need strength to fight sickness! You need energy to survive! The highest, enormously strong Power exists! Indeed! People named it God. It doesn't matter what is the name of this power! You must find your own connection with this Source of Energy, with God!"

Did You Ever Have the Chance to Marry an American Multimillionaire?

Books about this subject were forbidden in the Soviet Union. They could only be found in underground literature. But Della searched and grabbed any information about the possibilities of our body and mind, and it didn't matter in what form it was available: photocopied or handwritten sheets, small booklets, whatever. Unprofessional translators translated most of this information from English. Through friends she found some brochures about Yoga. With its philosophy, incompatible to the Soviet ideas and traditional science, Yoga was not popular at all, but Della started to practice it.

Reading and reading again, trying to follow every technique or exercise, she became lost in an ocean of different advice. Accidentally (or intuitively) she chose two pages with an Indian technique, named Kriya Yoga, feeling that it might help her more than others.

She was supposed to say a prayer with a list of Indian names, which she couldn't even pronounce, to do some exercises and then breathe in a special way. The technique was easy to do and Della practiced it for half a year or more. Little by little her health became better. She returned to her job. A mess in the Soviet Union pushed her to think about emigration. She forgot about Kriya Yoga and other techniques.

Here, in America, continuing her search for God, she participated in services of different synagogues; she tried Orthodox and Conservative congregations. Herbert brought her to a Reform temple, Temple Emmanuel, and she finally became a member of this temple.

It was her religion, her place. She was among her people, feeling comfortable with them. But they prayed in Hebrew. Della barely knew English, and didn't know Hebrew at all. She prayed and didn't understand what she was praying for; her mind refused to make translations from Hebrew to English and from English to Russian. Hebrew became a barrier.

Once a friend invited Della to the Temple of Self Realization Fellowship. She listened to their prayers. All the Indian names of Gurus from her forgotten Russian prayers became alive. She could see their pictures on the wall.

Unbelievable! Life brought Della to the source of Kriya Yoga. She almost forgot about this breathing exercise that helped her to survive many years ago in Odessa. Now she found herself in the heart of Kriya Yoga. Indeed, the circle of life is unpredictable!

It was so timely. Tremendous stress of emigration, adjusting to a new country, plus sadness because of her broken relationship with Herbert exhausted Della. She desperately needed a new shot of energy. Kriya Yoga again was available to her, only now it was accompanied with the highest scientific level of teaching.

Della did not remember if she talked with Herbert about Kriya Yoga. Perhaps not. He wouldn't have accepted it. She continued to go to Temple Emmanuel Sabbath services less regularly. She more often attended the Self Realization Fellowship (SRF) Temple. Being there, learning, listening, and meditating helped her to deal with her loneliness. It was not easy, not at all.

A new 1998 year was approaching. The first time during her six years in America she was by herself, without Herbert, felt terribly sad and lonely. SRF Temple offered a New Year's Eve meditation. She came to the Temple, she came to God. Alone. The joy was indescribable. It was the best New Year's Eve in her entire life.

At home she looked at Herbert's picture:

"God was with me this evening, I wish you, dear Herbert, all the happiness in the world."

CHAPTER 47

A MILLION TIMES she mulled over what went wrong in their relationship. Later she understood: nothing went wrong. Their break-up was not a failure. It was the opposite; it was a growth. For Della that break-up was the opportunity to look at what she was and what she wanted. God sent Herbert to Della to help her to go through the process of immigration. Now he left. His job was done. She gained a deeper understanding of herself, her likes and dislikes. She became single again. Getting to know yourself was a great gift of being single.

Busy with daily activities, Della somehow handled her life, but at night all the feeling became unleashed. At night she was choked with memories, pain, and disappointments. She felt if she did not do anything with this inner tenseness she would experience a volcanic explosion in her mind and she couldn't predict in what direction it would go. It was such a strong, persevering pressure that Della was afraid of this. All her inner-self commanded: "Do something!"

Her memories yelled, cried, claimed to be free from the old rust. These memories refused to be in her mind's jail.

She didn't know what to do and started to journal. She didn't think how to write, in English or in Russian, she just let the flow spill out from her. To her surprise the flow came out in English words. She wrote many stories.

The newspaper *The San Diego Jewish Times* announced a "MEMORY" Contest. Della sent them two of her stories. Several weeks later the editor of this newspaper called Della and told her that one of her stories won the Second Prize, the other one received Honorable Mention. Wow! She won the Second Prize among American writers throughout all of San Diego County. With her limited English. Impossible! Incredible! This could not happen!

No, it was reality. Della's story was chosen. She was invited for the ceremony to receive her award. They took photos of her. She also was asked to bring her pictures of the time the story was about.

Several weeks later the newspaper came with her photos, her story, and short biographical paragraph. She looked at her story printed in English in an American newspaper and at her pictures. She couldn't believe her eyes. Della never was published in Russia. She was only five years in the USA, an elderly woman who dared to write articles and stories in the almost unknown for her second language.

During all these years Della was accustomed to share with Herbert all happy and sad events that had happened in her life. Now she felt the strong necessity to share this success with him. She talked to herself: *stop it, don't do it, he is not interested in you anymore, he lives with another woman, forget about him, don't show anything to him.*

Della had classes in college, she took her car and drove in the direction of college; she did not know how, but her wheels turned to Herbert's office.

She walked inside. The office was in a new place, very well styled. There was a woman who quietly sat in the corner of the office. Della understood that it was Herbert's new Russian girlfriend he lived with. Herbert was walking around the room trying to find or to organize something. When he turned and saw Della, his face lit up. He was so glad to see her. She noticed a huge, also new, beautiful leather armchair in his office. Della sat in his armchair. Now Herbert didn't have a place to sit and stood near Della.

"Good," she thought inside, "I will sit in your armchair and you will stand near me, as you always did. Yes, definitely standing near me is your place."

Della noticed the newspaper with her story on his desk. Aha, it looked like Herbert already knew that she won the contest. How did he know so fast? The newspaper came only yesterday.

"I just finished reading your story in the newspaper. My daughter received the newspaper and ran to show it to me. You did a beautiful job, I am proud of you."

Did You Ever Have the Chance to Marry an American Multimillionaire?

"Thank you. I am proud of myself also."

"Why did you win only the second prize, not the first?"

"You become jealous, my darling. You should not carry envy inside of you. You have a beautiful woman near you now. By the way, why did you put her in the very far corner of your office? Shame on you."

Della joked, sitting in his huge armchair in the middle of his office and feeling as if she was seated on a throne.

"Introduce her to me, please."

He jumped obliging as always, and ran to Della.

"This is Ales, my new girlfriend."

He felt uncomfortable standing. He couldn't tell Della to stand up and to give him the armchair.

Della gallantly bowed her head to Herbert:

"I am so proud of you with your choice."

Della looked at this woman: nice looking with short haircut. She noticed her black hair color. Herbert didn't push her to be "Lucy Red." He became tired of that stupid experiment with Della. Now the color of this girlfriend's hair was not important for him. He had too much in his mind to think about.

"Nice to meet you, Ales."

Della didn't name herself; there was no reason to. Ales knew exactly her name and who Della was. She started to talk with her in Russian.

"Where are you from?"

"From Moscow."

"How long are you here?"

"Five years."

"Oh, you have more experience than I had when I met him. I was only three months in America. So, you took my place in his condo."

"Yes, it looks that way."

"How do you feel with him?" They continued to talk in Russian.

"For now it is okay."

"I am glad for you. I felt terrible in his condo. It was for me like a dark prison and I finally ran away to New York. You look younger than me."

"I am 52."

"He is 76. The difference in the age is almost a quarter of a century. He is very rich, but he won't give you a penny."

She became angry with Della and immediately changed Russian to English.

"I live with him not because of money," she made this declaration in English giving Herbert opportunity to understand her altruistic affirmation.

Della laughed, looked at Herbert and translated for him in English what she said in Russian.

"I told Ales in Russian that you are very rich and would never give her money. I told her that we broke up because of your damn money."

"T-s-s... What was between us, nobody should know. Be quiet, please."

"Okay, whatever you say. Everything is just for you."

Many times Herbert told Della these words. Now it was her turn to repeat this phrase to him with humor.

Della rose up from his huge comfortable leather armchair, looked at Herbert laughing. He looked at her and started to laugh also.

"You are something. I like you."

Della came to him closer, hugged him, looked in his eyes, and said just into his ear:

"No, you don't like me. You love me very much. You will always compare to me any woman who will be near you. You will always dream about me. You love me more than anybody on the Earth."

Herbert became serious. He kissed her eyes and whispered in her ear:

"Yes, I do. You are right."

Della left. She didn't know that he was already mortally sick. She didn't know that the next time he would hug and kiss her he would be condemned to death. She didn't know anything. It was their last meeting while he was still in good shape and he hugged her and kissed her, in spite of the presence of his new girlfriend.

CHAPTER 48

DELLA CAME HOME feeling like a dead fish on the beach without water.

"Why did you go to him? What did you lose in his office? Can you forget about him forever? It is over. Don't belittle yourself, never ever think about him. He looks happy, he already sleeps with another woman. They both look peaceful. Why did you appear near him? Did you want to boast with your article in the newspaper? Big deal! Throw away him from your mind! Forever! Finally you are free. You are in America, you know English, your article won a prize, you have a computer you can do your writing. You can do everything that you want to. Just do it."

Easy to say. Della felt Herbert's vibrations and couldn't get rid of them. She knew he also thought about her, fighting with himself inside.

We never know how we will end the old relationship and what will happen afterwards. Deepak Chopra, who has written many books about us, human beings, said: "If something doesn't go in your way, there is a reason. Trust your fate. Trust God. Forgive, and let it go."

Actually, Della followed this advice. She forgave Herbert and let him go. She was brave during the day time. Then nights came and she couldn't sleep.

In the middle of one of the sleepless nights Della left her bed, went to computer, opened it, and typed:

> "Did you ever have a chance to marry an American Millionaire?"

She inserted the date: January 26, 1998. Then she deleted the word Millionaire and typed Multimillionaire.

Now a new title appeared:

"Did you ever have a chance to marry an American Multimillionaire?"

That was all, she couldn't continue. She was blank. Only heavy sadness was inside of her. This heaviness blocked her entirely. She saved this title; Della had no idea what she would do with it. There was only a title. She closed her computer, went back to bed and fell asleep immediately.

The days ran by. We can make our firm decisions, but how do we make ourselves strong enough to handle these brave decisions? Depression came. Della was filled with pain and sadness even though she made herself busy as much as she could. English and computer classes in college, performances in the Senior Stage Academy, gym, pool, meditations at the Self Realization Fellowship. Deadly tired in the evening, she couldn't sleep again.

She prayed: "Dear God, I know You won't give me more than I can handle. I just wish you did not trust me so much."

Her brain continued its unstoppable spinning. She knew that keeping a journal could help. She pushed herself to write in a notebook or dictate in a tape recorder to get this painful stuff out of her system. She permitted the thoughts to flow their own way and did not want to control them; she did not want to check the grammar and spelling. Right now it was only important to let out whatever flowed from her. She did not know what thoughts would jump out from her mind in next minute.

Della asked herself: "What forces me to write? What is the strong power inside of me that keeps me awake in the middle of the night, pulls me out of my cozy bed and pushes me to the computer? What for?"

She was not sure if she would give it to anybody to read. She was just not able to resist this force.

Did You Ever Have the Chance to Marry an American Multimillionaire?

Really, what is the writing? Is it some kind of energy that needs to be explored and then released? Sometimes it felt like a painful archeological dig to explore an old injury. Or was this energy so strong because Della had overgrown her shell? It was a tremendous need she had inside. It was joyful in one way, it was very painful in another way. Della felt herself too vulnerable and sensitive, she definitely needed protection. Was this writing somehow her solace and support? Maybe.

She typed her thoughts out, felt released, and went back to sleep like a baby... until new thoughts and ideas come from her subconscious and asked to be freed. And she did. She needed to do it to feel better and to release them from her system.

Della knew that many good writers experienced the same feelings.

Who knows, maybe this general anxiety means suffering labor pains? Why do we need to explore painful areas of our life? Why do we need to rummage through old wounds? Do we really exorcize ghosts as we write down our memories? Do we open up the Pandora's Box inside of us? Who knows?

Della just knew that she couldn't not do it. She must, she had to put her thoughts on the page whatever reason pushed her to do it. Maybe, depression blanketed her as she relived old trauma, but she didn't care. She knew that it was the only way for her to feel inner freedom. If so, bless this depression!

When she woke up in the morning feeling doomed in some way, she knew it came from creative labor pains and she must accept it.

CHAPTER 49

THE YEAR 1998 continued its way. Time ran fast. It was October already. Della came to her bank and stood in line. It was also Herbert's bank; he brought Della here many years ago. The bank's manager knew that Della had been in a long relationship with Herbert; she also knew that they had broken up and now he lived with another Russian woman. The manager was busy with a customer, but when she saw Della, she got up from her chair and came to Della and took her aside. She asked Della:

"Do you know about Mr. Samson?"

"What happened?"

"Oh, he is very, very sick. He has a tumor in his brain."

"What?"

"Yes, and it is not operable."

The manager couldn't talk with Della; she was very busy with customers. But anyway she quickly informed Della that Mr. Samson's biopsy showed a vast brain cancer. Doctors couldn't do anything with it, it was too late. They sent him home.

A dark wave of sorrow rose in Della's whole body, pain for him, pain for herself. Brain tumor. Awful. It was old, maybe, it grew out over several years. Now she understood the cause of his strange behavior. Her Herbertchik was sick. Damaged brain? Having this diagnosis he behaved excellent, Della shouldn't have complained.

She rushed to Herbert's condo. The door was open, only the screen was locked. She rang the bell. A woman came to the screen. In her face Della saw hesitation. This woman didn't have any desire to let Della in. Della demanded with steel in her voice:

"Open! I have the right to come in."

The woman let Della in. Herbert was sitting on the sofa, dressed as usual. He was even wearing shoes. Resting at home, he never wore slippers,

Did You Ever Have the Chance to Marry an American Multimillionaire?

only shoes. Della noticed this detail and a thought flashed in her mind: "Things are not so terrible. He looks much better than I expected."

She sat near him on the sofa. He hugged her, whispering in her ears: "I love you."

He clung closer, repeating like a spell:

"I love you, I love you so much. You don't know how I love you!"

He snuggled up to Della, kissing every cell of her face. She kissed him, cuddled up to him as she wanted instinctively to give him her energy, to make him alive.

"I love you!" he repeated again and again. "I love you. I always loved you. You were a bright shiny sun for me, and I was just a little dull candle near you."

Della cried: "My Herbertchik, my Herbertchik, my Herbertchik!" She became somewhat hysterical:

"What did you do with your life? I asked you to get out from this condo! I asked you to go to the doctor. You did not listen to me. You are so stubborn, so stupid. A stupid idiot!"

Della was not able to stop her hysterics. She beat his chest with her fists: "You are so stupid, so stupid!" Della kissed him, soothing him, hugging, crying, touching. She knew she couldn't change anything. Desperate helplessness, an awful pain for his childish cowardice, for his resistance to go to the doctors choked her. He was on his mortal path. She didn't want to believe it, kissing him and repeating again and again:

"Why you did not listen to me? What did you do with your life?"

He whispered sadly: "I don't know. Whatever will be, will be. I only know that I have never loved anybody in my life like I love you."

"I know, I know, I know. Why am I not near you now? Why did you not listen to me? What did you do with your life? Why I am not near you now?" She repeated all these crying, yelling, being unable to control herself.

Della didn't want to believe that he was dying. She couldn't take it. It was beyond her understanding.

The woman made her presence known. They forgot about her. She told Della in Russian:

"Be careful, he had a biopsy on his head."

Della looked at the back of his head. It was a wound, covered with the bandage. Della didn't know who this gray woman was.

"Where is Ales?" Della asked her.

"I am Ales."

Della didn't recognize her. Herbert had introduced Ales to Della about half a year ago. She had changed tremendously.

"How long did the doctors say he would be alive?"

"About three months."

Herbert interrupted their Russian conversation. He scrutinized Della.

"You look good!"

"Thank you."

He again and again looked at Della.

"You really look so good."

He sadly sighed and stood up.

She clung to him feeling his heart beat.

"Oh, Dellishka, you are constantly with me. I do not remember a minute that you were not somewhere in my mind. It is not easy to forget our four, no, five years together. I always think about you. I remember everything. Yes, you are in my mind constantly."

"The same is with me. Herbertchik, I am not only in your mind, I am in your heart. So are you in my heart. I will be always with you."

"Whatever will be with me, will be. I love you so much," he whispered.

He looked at Della again. She was near him, his woman, whom he couldn't surpass in this life. He was smart. He understood that he lost his life game. He was a failure. He couldn't outwit life. He couldn't take it.

He hugged her again, kissing her. She didn't know that it was his last touch, last embrace. She didn't know that they would be parting forever. He knew.

Della couldn't bring herself to leave, she just stood there staring at him, wanting to drink him all in, to hold on to all of it, to feel his still strong hands, to look in his eyes. His words were whisper soft... "I love you so much..." He escorted her to the door, showing her that she was supposed to leave.

She kissed him goodbye and left.

She came home, her throat was choked, she couldn't do anything, flinging herself around in her apartment, thinking again and again that he knew that something serious was going on with him. Yes, he knew. Herbert, a man with such a strong personality, was simply afraid to face the reality that his sickness could be cancer. He was a great businessman. Not everybody could make millions without a penny to begin with. But he felt very insecure inside, instinctively increasing his money to feel more powerful. Actually, his making money was a form of running away from himself.

Ales said that he was going to live about three months. What is really going on with Herbert? Della needed more information and called Clint.

Clint already knew that Della saw Herbert. Ales called him immediately after she left. Clint explained to Della that he was going to take Herbert to the radiologist on Thursday.

Della said to him:

"This tumor started to grow a long time ago. It changed his personality. It was the cause of our breakup."

"You are right," he replied. "I also couldn't get along with him."

"I know. Herbert told me that he broke with you. Please let me know how he feels. Also I know him much better than Ales. Can I be near him?"

"Thank you. I will call you if anything will be needed," Clint said.

In the evening Herbert's oldest stepson Al, the lawyer, called Della from Los Angeles.

"Della, please don't come to Herbert anymore. His health situation is strictly a family matter."

Was it an order? Did he forbid her to see Herbert on his mortal passing? Who cares? Why should Della obey?

CHAPTER 50

THE NEXT MORNING Della prepared stuffed cabbage that Herbert liked very much and came to his condo. The door was locked. She left the food near the door and called Herbert later. Instead of Herbert, Ales picked up the phone. She said that in the morning something wrong happened to Herbert, that his son Clint called the doctor, and they decided to take Herbert to hospice.

"Hospice? Ales, you told me that the doctor said he would live at least three months."

"Yes, I did. But this is what happened this morning. Herbert jumped out from the condo in his underpants. His next door neighbor came into her car and started it. Herbert fought with her trying to take the keys from the woman's hands and tried to sit in the driver's seat, shouting "I must go to Della!" The engine was on, it could have caused an accident. The woman shouted for help and, thank God, another man was near and took Herbert out of her car."

Della stood near the telephone paralyzed.

"Herbert did it, such an intelligent man? Unbelievable!"

"Yes, he did. I immediately called Clint."

"Ales, yesterday Al called me from Los Angeles. He forbade me to see Herbert. I was surprised."

"Did he? Yesterday after you left I called Clint."

"I like Clint and I like Al. We had a nice relationship when I was with Herbert. Try to keep yourself calm, Ales. I know it is hard. It is not easy for me either. You need to take care of yourself."

Della sighed sadly. Did my visit cause this hospice? Is it my fault? Oh, no, dear God, please, not this. Was it too painful for Herbert to see me? But how could I not come to him? God, forgive me, please."

Did You Ever Have the Chance to Marry an American Multimillionaire?

All Della's body became frozen. She couldn't even cry. Her tears disappeared.

She begged herself: *Cry, please, cry...* She couldn't. Her tears were burned out, her eyes were dry.

Della desperately tried to understand what was going on in her life, with Herbert, with herself. Della's dear man, the greatest person she met once in her lifetime, was dying. She was unable to help him. She knew that everything is a lesson. What lesson should she derive here? Does God give us pain as a great teacher, as a lesson we should go through?

"God, dear, dear God, why did You do this to Herbert? Why does he have this tumor, for what sin? Only for helping me and Rachel he deserves to be healthy. Dear God, please, forgive him. Please, God, let me be near him, let me be near him, please... Please, find the way to give him everything he needs now. He is very lonesome and insecure. With all his millions. How can his account help him now? His money is nothing for him now. Nothing!!! Absolutely nothing... Please, let him go with less pain and suffering."

Why are people so attached to money? So stupid. People, not God, created money. They did it to please themselves, to compete with themselves, to feel the power. People fight for money. Money brings happiness; money brings sorrow. Who knows what comes more with money? Joy or grief?

Della called Clint asking permission to visit Herbert in hospice. The answer was: "Sorry, no."

This was the end. A single person is missing for you and the whole world is empty. It seemed to Della that if she would be able to collect all the compliments, delight, and admiration that Herbert offered her during all the years they were together, it would be nothing compared to how this man glorified her in his eyes and in her own.

She didn't cry, she couldn't. Her tears were suppressed deep inside. An excruciating, unbearable, enormous pain in every cell of her body tore her apart, her soul cried, but not her eyes. Tears would be a blessing for her, but her eyes forgot about tears.

⁂

Herbert and Della discovered for themselves an affirmation: *Dance with God in life*. Della repeated it often. We can have God, we can pray to Him and ask Him to guide us. But now Della was beaten. She felt herself on the anvil.

God will come, put us on the anvil,
And beat us, and beat, and hold,
Until our inner plain copper
Will be transformed into pure gold.

Where to find the strength to dance with God? How? With a heart full of pain?

⁂

"Dear Herbertchik, you are in hospice now. You pressed the button with the final sign "Down!" and your elevator rapidly rushes you to the basement."

Herbert knew this; it didn't matter if he was conscious or unconscious, he was already not here and not there yet.

Right now he goes through his own hell or… relief. Yes, relief. He made all his decisions, he burned all his boats; he had no way back.

He lost Della, children, his millions, his condo that he was attached to so tightly. He didn't need Della's signature on his prenuptial agreement that became just a piece of junk paper ready to go into the garbage. Della will keep it for a while like a souvenir, then will not know what to do with

Did You Ever Have the Chance to Marry an American Multimillionaire?

it. She will also keep the tons of pictures Herbert took of her. With time she will push aside all the albums on the shelf and later wouldn't also know what to do with them. All stuff that is so worthy for us when we are alive becomes nothing when we are ready to leave this world.

The elevator of Herbert's life rushes to the bottom and what will happen when it stops?

Nobody knows. Herbertchik, perhaps you feel that you are rushing to hell, to a deep trap-hole. Hopefully, it will be not a dark bottom, but an open wide window with a bright light ahead. Now you won't be afraid of this light in the window. Let this light shine above and around you. You will see a green meadow with a soft aromatic carpet of flowers, a sunny expanse where you will find a way into a new... dimension. Dance with God, Herbertchik! Dance with God!

CHAPTER 51

OCTOBER 29, 1998. Early morning. Della barely slept all night, fighting with sorrowful thoughts. She was not able to put herself in any positive mood, feeling so stupidly powerless, paralyzed. She felt like somebody put on her a heavy stone, a rock, a mountain. Della couldn't move under it, she barely breathed.

Della was not a psychologist. She just was very curious, what power attaches people on the vibrational level even when they don't want it. All those days, knowing that Herbert was dying, she did her best not to let this heavy sense arise in her, purposely participating in many activities, actually running away from home and from herself not to be alone with her thoughts. But Herbert existed in her mind constantly.

In this particular morning, terribly exhausted, Della gave up. She permitted herself to do nothing, to not push herself toward anything. She decided to make this day the laziest day in her life. Actually, she didn't have another choice; she simply was not able to move. The heaviness she felt in her body and in her head was unbearable, she will remember it forever. She put on the TV, found the International Channel. The time for Russian news was from 12:30 PM till 1:30 PM. She watched this program, unsuccessfully trying to concentrate on the news from Moscow. She ate her lunch near the TV and didn't feel the taste of food that she swallowed and did not remember what she ate.

Usually after the Russian program they showed news from Poland, from 1:30 until 2:30 p.m. Absentmindedly looking on the screen, she did not even notice when the Russian program was over. Now they talked in Polish. Della sat in her armchair deadly tired. She said to herself: "Change the channel, you don't understand Polish." But she was not able to move a finger to click the remote control. She was crushed.

Suddenly in the middle of the Polish program, without any explanation, Della felt that she was released from that tremendous heaviness and gravity. The mountain above her disappeared.

Did You Ever Have the Chance to Marry an American Multimillionaire?

She jumped:

"I am free! I am free!!!"

She didn't know what had happened, why she felt so released. She jumped with joy. Good energy came back to her, and she was ready to do a thousand things. The time was around 2 o'clock in the afternoon.

In the evening Clint called her and said:

"Dad passed away at 2 o'clock this afternoon. Very peacefully. The funeral will be on November 2. I will call you about the time."

Now Della had an explanation. Until his last moment Herbert was tuned to Della and she felt the tremendously heavy energy of his thoughts, maybe on a subconscious level, because his brains were damaged with the vast tumor. He died and the heaviness was gone. Herbert died and Della felt released. Why? Perhaps because death, at last, was a release for Herbert.

Della felt the moment when he died! Incredible. Later Della asked knowledgeable people to explain this phenomena. She was given a scientific explanation: *"Matter is compressed energy, and energy is consolidated thought."* Too scientific, Della was not sure that she understood this. It just happened that Della was an open channel for Herbert's vibrations and his vibrations were so terribly sad that they choked Della.

If it is correct, Herbert's thoughts about Della in his death agony became so strongly materialized that Della physically felt their heavy pressure. This experience was horrible. If this is a reality, we better be taught how to avoid this extreme attack, how to protect ourselves from the influence of something invisible that affects our well being.

Clint said that Herbert left peacefully. Della prayed for this. Was it the answer to her prayers? If so, thank you, dear God.

―――

How do different circumstances appear in our life? Unexpected, so unpredictable that we never ever could imagine that it would happen to us. Suddenly something occurs that we need to deal with. On what level are all these events prepared for us? Is it only God's power and His will? Don't we build our fate? What is our part in our own destiny?

Herbert had brain cancer. Did God prepare for him such a monstrous punishment? Was it Herbert's Karma? A result of the sum of actions in his previous existences?

Actually, this is nothing new: interconnection between our actions and retribution for them has been well known in the East for more than a thousand years. Hindus believe that the day of reckoning will come. They assert that sickness is always a punishment for our unrighteous way of life, our attitudes and deeds.

Dear Herbert, what did you do wrong in your life? You always told Della that you worked very hard to make your money. She believed you, she knew you were not lazy. Who knows why you were given such a big torment?

Della tried to learn and to understand the meaning of our lives. What is truly lasting? What do we possess that we are able to take with us beyond this fleeting life? We can take only ourselves, our love and wisdom. Does the next life exist?

At least in this life, the brightest future is often based on a long forgotten past; we can't go forward in life until we let go our past failures and heartaches. Herbert is released. Go forward, Della!

CHAPTER 52

DELLA'S DEAR FRIEND Barbara kindly offered to be with Della at this sorrowful funeral day. She drove an hour from her home to support Della emotionally and to take her to the cemetery.

Trying to diminish her inner tension, Della jokingly asked her friend:

"Did you ever have the opportunity to be at the funeral of a multimillionaire?"

"No, never."

"Now you will have this experience. I came all the way from Russia to give you this chance."

They finally approached Shalom Mausoleum with a big Star of David on the building. Della met Herbert's relatives, whom she hadn't seen for a long time. They hugged Della and were very friendly. The coffin, made from simple natural unpainted pine, without any embellishments, was on the floor, not even on a pedestal. Herbert was a thin, tall man. The coffin was long and narrow. Is Herbert inside? Just 10 days ago he kissed her and didn't stop repeating: "I love you so much, oh, you cannot imagine how I love you." It sounded like a spell to let Della know that she should remember this forever.

Nobody's life goes smoothly. Life is not an easy journey. Probably, it looks like riding a huge heavy elephant. Dear Herbert, you had a great ride on your elephant, achieved a high position in American society, and became a successful, wealthy person. Alas, wealth is powerless in the face of sickness. God makes his own plans. We are all equal human beings in front of death.

According to Jewish tradition, we are not supposed to bring flowers to the funeral. Della did not want to accept this. With flowers we say a loving "Goodbye" to a deceased person. Della came to the ceremony with a basket of red roses. Herbert always presented red roses to her. Somebody took the basket from her hands and put it near the coffin.

Della whispered to herself again and again:

> *"God, grant me the serenity*
> *To accept things I cannot change,*
> *Courage to change the things I can,*
> *And wisdom to know the difference."*

"My dear Herbertchik, I cannot come to myself going through such deep grief and sorrow. It is extremely hard to handle such a huge emotional stress. Your loving encouragement helped me profoundly. You believed in me, and I promise, I swear, I will not disappoint you. In my memory you will always be alive."

Herbert's nephew, who was a rabbi, started the service.

"Baruch, Atou, Adonai, Eloheinu, Melech Ha'olum" - a prayer began in Hebrew.

Della looked at the plain wooden box with Herbert. It will never be opened, he would never stand up and kiss her and tell her how he loves her, she would never hear his voice, never ever see him again.

She was ready to jump and hug this box with him inside. She cried, now her tears found their way outside. She felt an excruciating pain for the impossibility to change anything. He was afraid to go to doctors and died so stupidly, without trying to help himself. Or maybe he wanted to die. She really understood how much she loved him, how dear he was to her.

"Dear Herbert," she whispered to herself, "you will be squeezed in a cold marble wall. Cold stone will become your home forever now, without any ray of sun and any twitter of birds. It is located very high in the wall, under the ceiling. You always were afraid of heights. Now an ironical fate has made you lie forever almost under the ceiling. You kept so many treasures in your soul and held so much beauty as a human being. You even didn't realize this. You were so blinded by your wealth.

"My dear Herbertchik, you opened in me the bottle with a powerful elixir of my personality. I didn't know my own abilities. You opened me up

Did You Ever Have the Chance to Marry an American Multimillionaire?

for my own growth, for my own good. I think I was an unsolved enigma in your life. If reincarnations are real, we should meet again in our next lifetime.

"You will be always in my memory: a strong man, successful businessman, with a very sensitive and sentimental soul who needed only love. This terrible sickness made you full of fears, it was not your fault. Forgive me, please, for anything that I did wrong to you. I know that we came to each other like a great reward. We had been a perfect match by soul and by our mind.

"Rest in peace, my beloved forever. You did the best you could in this masquerade show that we call LIFE. You are done. God wants me to continue my dance at this Masquerade. Sooner or later I will join you. It is inevitable."

After the funeral everybody was invited for a reception at Herbert's condo. The curtains were raised and the windows were opened. It was a sunny day outside and the condo looked very bright. Sad memories about the time when Della lived here attacked her.

Della did not have the opportunity to be near Herbert during his last days. He was isolated, maybe because any person who would appear near him could possibly take advantage of his money. He was cut off from everybody. His recent girlfriend, whom he asked to move into his home because he was unable to manage his loneliness, was sitting near him like a chained dog. She received an order not to let anybody come near him. Maybe to give him a rest? But this "a rest" literally looked to Della like "arrest."

Herbert was taken into custody in his own home. It was such a sad final stage of his life. His condo became a prison for him.

Somehow Della felt he **knew** for many years that it was his jail, but he didn't recognize it or was afraid to acknowledge it.

Della did not want to participate in this reception. Soon she left.

In the evening Ales called Della:

"I found your pictures. I want to give them to you. I cannot sleep in his condo. I am going now to my daughter. I will sleep in her house. Would you like me to stop by to your place?"

"Okay. I will wait for you downstairs near the pool."

Ales came, a shivering, tired woman, full of problems. Della felt compassion for her. She gave Della a thick packet with pictures and another little packet with cookies.

"These are left over from the party. I cannot eat sweets. I have diabetes. I am going to give some cookies to my daughter also."

Della took a cookie, chewing it mechanically. They talked quietly sitting near the blue pool. It was a very nice evening with a clear sky, full of stars.

Ales told Della:

"I cannot sleep in his place. I feel awful. Yesterday I took four sleeping pills, very strong. I have them from Russia. I never took so much at once. And I slept, maybe, two hours."

"You know, I couldn't sleep in his condo either. But I am very sensitive, it is my nature. I feel immediately the atmosphere in the house," Della said.

"You are right. Something is wrong in his condo."

"I felt heaviness there. The walls weighed me down. I struggled with this feeling and couldn't do anything. I thought, maybe it is because his old wife was sick a long time in this house and died in the bedroom where we slept. Perhaps her spirit was still around there."

"So, now she took him back."

"What are you going to do?" asked Della.

"I have no idea. I put myself on the waiting list in a government building for people with low income."

"Why did you decide to live with a man who was older then you almost a quarter of a century?"

"I liked him. I worked too hard. My health was not good. He took me away from my job; I rested and started to feel much better."

Did You Ever Have the Chance to Marry an American Multimillionaire?

"I believe you. He was a very nice person. I hope you had a chance to be happy with him."

"Yes, in the beginning it was a pleasure to be near him."

"Did you ever go together for a walk to the ocean during this year?"

"No, never."

"Yes, I know. He was afraid of the fresh wind blowing and the ocean. I fought with him. I couldn't live without the ocean and fresh air. It was a disaster for me.

"When I came to his home, he also forbade me to open the windows; I said that I would die without air.

"Now I think that perhaps he felt something uncomfortable in his head before the tumor in his brain appeared. He told me that he had skin cancer before and was afraid of the sun. He always wore a hat, trying to protect himself from sun and air-conditioning."

They hugged each other, two women who just buried the man who brought so much into their lives.

Della took the package with the pictures. Inside was an envelope bound with a rubber band. Herbert always put a rubber band on something very important to him. She opened this envelope. There were two of her pictures. One of them she brought from Russia. It embellished his fireplace over several years. Another one was made here, in America. Della had never seen it. She looked gorgeous in it. She thought:

He tied up these two of my pictures so thoroughly, with so much love. He tried to bury all memories about me; he took another woman in his bed, but he couldn't throw me away from his heart. He kept my pictures in his business envelope with the name of his very rich company.

There was his picture also. A gorgeous, handsome man. And this man is dead? Impossible! God, dear God, why do the best go away first?

"I found more pictures of him. I can give them to you," Ales said.

"Thank you, Ales, I don't want anything. It is over. I don't want to bother my memory. I wish you the very best in your life. From all my heart. Take a good care of yourself. You deserve it, dear Ales."

CHAPTER 53

Depression attacked Della. It was emptiness around, emptiness inside and outside. So big that for a few years she didn't know how to deal with herself. In her mind she again and again twirled their several years together. Herbert totally occupied her mind with his sincere love and his eyes full of admiration. She talked with him mentally and discussed any situation in her current life. He still remained her adviser. Angry at herself, she wanted to get rid of this tiresome delusion. Without her willing, Della became involved in the tremendously hard process of detaching herself from a person whose soul was bound up with her soul. She felt that she tore herself apart, but all her inner power was too weak to make this detachment.

She constantly told herself: "Nobody can make you happy if you choose to be unhappy. Nothing can make you unhappy if you choose to be happy." She repeated it thousand times. Did this affirmation work for her? Alas, she was unable to follow it.

The brain tumor changed Herbert. He broke with almost everybody from his family. He broke with Della. He was afraid to become close to anybody because he saw each person maneuvering for his money. Money controlled him, he became its slave.

Somewhere Della had heard: "The courage to be rich is a fascinating journey." It turns out that we need to be brave to have a big amount of money in the bank. We have to be strong enough to be able to handle this money, and not let it control us. So, maybe, it is easier to be poor? No, we create another problem in our brains. We want to be rich. We think that money will give us power and security. We spend each dollar very carefully.

Lugging all these thoughts became too tiring. Standing at the cusp of her life at age sixty, she knew she'd better conserve energy to start a new life without Herbert and without any man.

Della tried her best to calm down and make herself a new keep-cool persona. Continuing her intensive journal process, she learned that those who keep a journal recover from trauma as well as, or as soon as, those in therapy. It helps surviving humiliating moments. Della still did not know whether Herbert brought in her life more excitement or more sorrow. Now it was more suffering.

What Della understood: each of us goes in his own life's harness. Each of us should learn to play his own life's violin and order his own melody. If we wait for somebody to order the music for us and dance their music, we will be always dependent. If something is going wrong in our life, the cause is inside of ourselves: we think wrong thoughts, communicate with wrong people, eat wrong food and attach ourselves to wrong places.

Della wrote a lot, mostly in English. She hoped that the results of writing would be tremendously satisfying and beneficial for her, and maybe for other people, if she chose to publish some of her writings. She read somewhere that solitude and sadness produced geniuses. Creative work is their refuge. If so, Della will bless this depression!

Della was already six years in America. Thinking about these intensive six years in the United States, she wrote a poem.

The First Six Years in America

Who said that America is a paradise on this Earth?
At first we went through ordeal of a secondary birth.
Emigration was like a strong ice-cold shower
That forced all our strengths and inner power.

Without knowing any English sound,
We must understand what was going around,
Constantly praying to Saints of all religions
To assist us in these new life's collisions!

Did You Ever Have the Chance to Marry an American Multimillionaire?

Every new day brought another unknown test.
We didn't have time to breathe and to rest.
With all our senses we could keenly feel
How our skin was painfully peeled.

Emigration is not a fantastic Arabic fairy-tale.
Any time the best dreams and desires could fail.
We went through thousand and one sleepless nights,
Trying hard to look fearless and bright.

We were lost in American laws,
We dealt with emotional highs and lows.
Many years we dreamed about this beautiful land.
We were naive and built all dreams on the sand.

It didn't matter in what country we were born.
But what really matters is our inner horn.
We needed to know this country, to feel this ground.
We must be able to make many friends all around.

Emigration is not sweet honey.
It is not about to have more money.
It is a tremendously hard work for our soul,
It is a life storm, a long, strong thunder roll.

The Bible intends the seventh day for joy and rest.
On the seventh year we will breathe with full breast.
Hard times are gone and don't exist anymore.
Let us enjoy this life, breathe deeper, feel more.

It is a marvelously beautiful land.
I am ready to sink in its ocean's soft sand.
I send my children all love and light,
So bright they would see the sun at midnight.

I am proud I sang this American song of survival.
I am ready to bow in front of the Torah and Bible
Telling God a thousand thankful words
For the Heaven that was given to me in this world.

(Five years later Della will be invited to Orlando, Florida, where International Society of Poets will present a Merit Award, a Silver Cup, to Della Gordon for the poem "The First Six Years in America")

Della's journal became her catharsis. She wrote in her journal:

"My dear man, you were so rich and so poor. You could be the happiest person on the Earth, but you were not. God gave you everything to enjoy life. You were handsome, healthy, talented, energetic, smart. You did not waste your life; you became a multimillionaire. How many people can do it in their life? Only the chosen ones. God selected you to put in his circle. How did you use God's gift? You made borders and limits for yourself. You became poverty-stricken long before your sickness. Having a lot of money,

Did You Ever Have the Chance to Marry an American Multimillionaire?

you bought your small condo (not in a good area) many years ago, long before your sickness. Your subconscious thoughts worked only in one direction: to make money and to save. It became your inner need. You did not travel, you just made money, you saved money. The question is: for whom and for what? You continued to save when you already had so much that you wouldn't be able to spend it in your entire lifetime. Your children took it very negatively. You did not give anything to your relatives, nor to Della.

"Did you understand how much you missed in this life? You had the world opened widely for you. What pushed you to work so hard and to put all your money in the bank? When you were young you wanted to make money to be rich. You did it. So, what was the next step? To make money again to be more rich? You did it. You became richer. What was the next? The next was to hide from everybody that you were rich. Nobody was supposed to know about this. You wore casual clothes and drove an old car. It was a Cadillac, you didn't want to drive a small car, but that Cadillac was old. Your white gorgeous Lincoln did not belong to you. It belonged to the company.

"Almost nobody knew that you were the owner of your big shopping center. You hid it very carefully. You named yourself a "Manager", telling all your tenants that the real owner was your stepson Al in Los Angeles. Maybe it was somehow smart. You protected yourself from many pretensions and claims from your tenants. If it was a conflict, you gave Al's telephone to the complainer. Then the terrible sickness came and you left this world. My poor Herbertchik.

Nothing is truly learned until it is lived.

Della learned intensively. She established her own strategies for quieting her busy brain at night. Before even entering her bedroom she left all worries and concerns on the balcony outside the bedroom door. She read or listened to many tapes and books over the years. It's been amazing to her how a particular person or a smart book seemed to show up at the right time to give her the wisdom, direction, guidance, and understanding she needed. It helped her to believe she could do everything that her sweet soul desired. It brought into her awareness the courage to live without fear.

It is so terrific to be able to work toward harmony and love rather than finding fault and encouraging arguments. She didn't want to argue anymore. She has learned to love and to look through another pair of glasses at this wonderful life!

CHAPTER 54

A FEW YEARS passed. Della learned that the Internet can be a nice place to make friends. One gentleman, who introduced himself as Charles, lived in San Diego and invited her for lunch. They were sitting in a nice restaurant and peacefully talked as they waited for the food to arrive. He told Della that he had lived five years with a Russian woman. Then some deep disagreements interrupted their relationship. Della laughed:

"So, you had had an experience of five years with a Russian woman, and I had six years experience with an American man."

Della started to talk about Herbert. Then suddenly she found herself describing his death and her feelings. She told him that she felt the exact moment when he passed away. She interrupted herself:

"Why am I telling you such personal, secret things? I met you an hour ago; I never told this to anybody. I don't understand what pushes me to talk with you about this. Probably, it looks crazy in your eyes."

"No, I understand you. Go ahead, it is a fascinating story."

Without Della's will, her mouth and tongue continued to talk surprisingly openly to this man she barely knew.

"What am I doing?" she interrupted herself again. "I don't understand myself. Why do I feel so keenly the desire to talk about this with you? I must shut my mouth immediately!"

But she kept on talking about her sacred feelings and mentioned Ales. Suddenly this man asked:

"What was the name of your boyfriend?"

Della told him Herbert's name.

"My ex-girlfriend has a sister-in-law. Her name is Ales and she lived about ten months with an American who died from brain cancer. I have a hunch that it was the same man."

"Does this Ales have two daughters?"

"Yes, and he didn't get along with them. They didn't like him."

"Yes, I had heard this."

They checked some details that they knew about this story. They both became curious. Charles said:

"I have pictures of him. He was with Ales at our big party. Would you like to come to my house and to see the pictures?"

"Yes, I would. Can we do it right now? It is interesting."

"Yes, we can."

"Let us go!"

They went to his house. Della glanced at the pictures. Yes, it was Herbert.

"It looks like Herbert waves to me from his grave," Della said.

Charles offered, "You can take some photos, I have extra."

"No, thank you. I won't take any. I don't need his pictures anymore."

Then he told Della, "When relatives asked Ales to leave Herbert's forsaken condo she went to her daughter. She couldn't live with her and we invited her to live here, in my house. Now my ex-girlfriend bought her own house and Ales leaves with her."

He showed Della the room where Ales resided. Her mail still came to his address.

Della was amazed by the power that pushed her so persistently to describe intimate feelings of her private life with Herbert to a man who came to her from the computer's screen just today. Both Della and Charles were astonished. Was it an amazing coincidence? No, there are no coincidences in life.

CHAPTER 55

Two people talk.

One says: "I am a gambler."

The second asks: "Where are you gambling, on the computer?"

"No. In life. Life is a gamble. Each moment I make a choice and have no idea what the result will be."

Life is a swing. We push on the seat and the rope to go up, up, and then at some point we go down, and then up again. But we need to push. This is our responsibility.

Life is a show. Who created this show for each of us?? We, ourselves, or another power beyond us? Do we name this power God? Do we know exactly what the right name is of this incredible power?

Della realized that she was bringing to a close a large transitional chapter of her life and must make the next step. Everything is possible in this life. To dwell on the past? No way! The brightest future comes to an open mind.

Later in her life Della will be in another touching relationship. It will become the next very moving love story between two mature people, experienced in life: man and woman.

Age? Age is a case of mind over the matter. If you do not mind, it doesn't matter. Age offers blessed opportunity-after-opportunity to soar in whatever manner one's health and attitude permits, and continuously to learn to "make hay" by gathering the wisdom while the sum of opportunities shines in life.

Money? No doubt, it is great to have money.

But what does really matter? Our spirit. We must improve it and develop it continuously during our lifetime. It is our main obligation.

THE SPIRIT! THIS IS OUR DIVINE BANK ACCOUNT! UNLIMITED!

About the Author

DORA KLINOVA is an award-winning writer and poet. In 1992, Dora Klinova emigrated from her native homeland, Odessa, and left behind everything familiar, including her profession as an engineer-designer in the movie industry. By necessity, this life-changing event caused her to recreate herself and her world. Dora's thoughts and ideas flooded out onto paper like a rushing stream. To her own surprise, the torrent of words was in English, not her native Russian.

Her first book, *A Melody from an Immigrant's Soul* is heartfelt story of a soul who comprehends the symphonies of Russian and American life and fully appreciates all their musical notes. The book is all around the world now: from Australia and Japan, India, Brazil and Israel, to all of Europe, Canada and the United States.

Her second book, *The Queen of the Universe. The Vortex of Creation*, is a many-layered thoughtful allegory, a fable enlightening for adults and children alike. People of any age who are interested in gaining insight and spiritual growth will derive knowledge. *The Queen of the Universe* was published twice with different design and different illustrations. Also a video was made from this book.

Did You Ever Have the Chance to Marry an American Multimillionaire?

Dora's stories were selected for the anthology *Hot Chocolate for Seniors,* that was named gold medal and gold seal in 2012 International book Awards.

Many of Dora's works have been published in the *San Diego Union Tribune,* the *San Diego Jewish Times, The San Diego Jewish World,* and other newspapers and magazines in San Diego and New York. Selected pieces were performed at San Diego's Old Globe Theater, Old Town Theater and other theaters in San Diego.

In March 2003, Dora Klinova received a Silver Cup, Merit Award, from International Society of Poets for her poetry.

The Merit Award from International Society of Poets

The third Dora's book: *Did You Ever Have a Chance to Marry an American Multimillionaire?* was successfully previously published in color. Below is its image. The book you are holding in your hands is its second edition.

Made in the USA
San Bernardino, CA
14 July 2016